Relationship Remedies
Relating Better to Yourself and Others

Sam Owen

Names and identifying characteristics of people in the book have been changed to protect the privacy of the individuals.

Copyright © Sam Owen 2012 & © Saima Owen 2012

The right of Saima Owen to be identified as the author of this work has been asserted by her in accordance with the Copyright, Designs and Patents Act 1988.

All rights reserved. No part of this book may be photocopied, reproduced, stored in an information retrieval system (other than for purposes of review), published, performed in public, adapted, broadcast, transmitted or recorded without the prior written permission of the copyright owner.

British Library Cataloguing-in-Publication Data

A catalogue record for this book is available from the British Library.

ISBN: 978-0-9571635-0-8

Published by Saima Owen

Cover design by Philip Owen

Printed and bound by CPI Group (UK) Ltd, Croydon, CR0 4YY

NOTE: The author shall not be held liable for any loss or expense incurred as a result of relying on information stated within this book. The material contained within this book has been written in good faith as a general guidance.

This book is dedicated to my amazing parents for sharing their wisdom, and to my wonderful husband, the rest of my family and my dearest friends. Without you my life would be incomplete.

Contents

Chapter 1
Introduction 9

Chapter 2
The Basics 13

Chapter 3
The Blueprint 24

Chapter 4
Thoughts, Feelings And Behaviour 30

Chapter 5
Release The Handcuffs 40

Chapter 6
A Lesson Learned 46

Chapter 7
Forgive 54

Chapter 8
Stuck Like Glue 59

Chapter 9
The Fence Is Too High 65

Chapter 10
That's What You Said But... 74

Chapter 11
Your Hands Are Shouting At Me! 85

Chapter 12
Is It Me Or Is Everything Red? 98

Chapter 13
Changing Without Aggravating 109

Chapter 14
The Role You Are Playing 126

Chapter 15
Silently Loud 132

Chapter 16
I'm Not Psychic! 139

Chapter 17
Why Didn't I Realise Sooner? 153

Chapter 18
Relationships And Attraction – The Other Kind 165

Chapter 19
Don't Get Washed Away 194

Chapter 20
For Best Results Bake Until Risen 204

Chapter 21
Feel Your Way 212

Appendix 228

References 229

Chapter 1
Introduction

"The happiest people in the world are those who feel absolutely terrific about themselves, and this is the natural outgrowth of accepting total responsibility for every part of their life."

- Brian Tracy

It is likely that you have decided to read this book because you want some no nonsense advice on how to improve at least one important relationship in your life, whoever that may be with. After all, you know that your life's journey, your happiness and your successes along the way are all dependent upon the relationships you cultivate with yourself and others.

Some people seem to have successful relationships with everyone they meet, right? They have a natural flair for drawing people towards them and are often seen surrounded by laughing, smiling, happy people. At the other end of the spectrum, though, are those who struggle to even maintain the simplest of connections with another human being. The good news is that you can choose where on that spectrum you stand. The happiness of the laughing, smiling, happy bunch can be attained with a little know-how and effort combined with consistence and persistence. As with any endeavour, there will be an adjustment period where you have to actively concentrate on implementing more productive thoughts and behaviours in order to achieve your desired results but, given time, you will become the habits you have purposefully created.

The advice contained within this book does not simply sound great in theory. Its practical application will produce positive results. Here you will discover numerous insights and simple-to-apply tips to create the relationships you want in your life. This will lead you towards a happier, more fulfilling life experience and success at home and in your career. It may be that you are struggling with a particular relationship or that you are seeking help with the way you relate to people on the whole. Either way, here you will learn about the fundamentals for relating skilfully with other human beings.

To help you get the most out of this fulfilling journey there are "Action Points" included within this book. They provide you with an opportunity, and instruction, to reflect upon your own experiences *and* to take action to improve your situation.

*** Regardless of whether you are going to perform the Action Points as you read the book or return to complete them later, **you must read the exercises *as* you read the rest of the book**. They are significant to the chapters themselves. This is absolutely necessary as without them you will have missed vital information. ***

Everyone is different and as such we all have different ways of doing things. You know how you work best. I trust you to decide how best to use this book in a way that suits you. Therefore, listed here are three ways in which you can ensure you get the most out of this book whilst still working in a way that fits your personality:

- You can perform each exercise as you read your way through the book.
- Alternatively, you may wish to read this book from start to finish before you perform each of the important exercises within it.
- Chances are some of you will do a bit of both. You can do that too!

For the best results simply ensure you do definitely at some point commit to performing each effective exercise within this book if you are serious about achieving the relationship(s) that you desire.

As you read on you will notice that this book looks at the subtleties of relating and communication. Amending these subtleties will not have a profound effect overnight, but rather, over time. The current states of your relationships did not come about overnight either. They too came about over time. So give it time, watch how the smallest changes alter your relationships for the better and keep on building on those successes.

It is the ongoing patterns that you build and the ongoing love, trust, respect, friendship, commitment and communication that you demand *and* offer that is integral to your relationship outcomes. Relationships evolve. We too evolve whilst in those relationships. How you and your relationships evolve is dependent upon you and the choices you make. I'll repeat that. How you and your relationships evolve is dependent upon you and the choices you make.

By implementing new patterns consistently over a period of time you will elicit the types of relationships you desire. This will in turn feed your thoughts about your own self worth and your own capabilities. This will serve as a self-confidence boost and subsequently spill over into the relationships you have with others. Bouncing back and forth the positive experiences you create will nurture your relationship with yourself and others.

This book will help you to take full responsibility to change what is not working. Life is about taking responsibility. The experience of living the life you have always dreamed of far outweighs the momentary pleasure derived from blaming other people and other factors. To progress anything, your career, your wealth, your health or your relationships, ownership is the key. You are the driving force behind your own life experience.

Chapter 2

The Basics

"We can never obtain peace in the outer world until we make peace with ourselves."

- Dalai Lama

The first step in any journey is establishing where you want to go. You cannot board a plane or take a taxi without a destination in mind. If you do, you will waste your time, money and energy. Life is that way too. You need to know your destination. Whether that is the physical and mental place you want to be in a month, three months or three years, you need to know where your life compass is set for. Of course, in this instance we are talking about how and where you see yourself in terms of your relationships, be that with yourself and/or others. The two are inextricably linked so let us first start with your relationship with yourself.

To explore the idea of a healthy relationship with one's self, personality theories developed within the field of psychology provide some useful insights. Gordon Allport, an American psychologist born at the end of the 19th century, helped pioneer what is referred to as personality psychology. He developed his theories based on the evaluation of individual behaviour and thought rather than that of groups.

Allport suggested that individuals with a healthy personality are motivated by conscious processes whilst unhealthy personalities are motivated by unconscious processes. During his career Allport (1961) highlighted six aspects of a healthy personality as he saw it.

The first is a non-egotistical person that involves himself in activities and problems that are not centred on himself. He is not a self-centred individual and deems social interest, family and spirituality as important elements of life. He summarised this first tenet as "Everyone has self-love, but only self-extension is the earmark of maturity". In other words, we all love ourselves, this is human nature, but it is the ability to look beyond ourselves and our own needs and desires that indicates that we are mature and psychologically healthy.

Allport described the second aspect as the ability to warmly relate to others with love and compassion. A psychologically healthy, mature person treats others with respect. He is aware that his needs and desires and hopes are similar to those of others. Mature personalities are able to love others without being possessive or selfish.

The third factor is self-acceptance, also referred to as emotional security. These people accept challenges as a part of life rather than dwell on them or become overly upset by them. Emotionally secure people accept themselves for what they are.

The fourth aspect of this healthy personality is a realistic perception of one's environment. The person is grounded in reality and does not alter it to fit his own desires.

The fifth is insight and humour. Psychologically healthy and mature individuals are self-aware and so do not point the blame towards others for their own flaws and wrongdoings.

The sixth and final aspect of a healthy and mature personality, as according to Allport (1961), is a unifying philosophy of life. In other words, people with such a personality (whether religious or not) have a clear view of the purpose of life resulting in a non-cynical outlook. Such people are non-prejudiced, moralistic and driven to help their fellow men.

Allport developed much of these six criteria based on his own life experiences as well as his observations of others. That in itself is something worth remembering as we navigate our way through our own lives. We learn, and ought to learn, about ourselves and who we are by evaluating our own thoughts, emotions and behaviours as well as those of others. Indeed, we can glean a lot by doing so, thereby reducing the number of mistakes we make. Positive role models can be a great way to learn about personality traits that are beneficial to ourselves *and* those around us. Such introspection and observation of others is vital for the ongoing good health of our own psyche. If we understand ourselves and how what we do impacts on others around us then we can make informed choices about our approach to our relationships.

Furthermore, Allport's six criteria can be viewed as key ingredients of not only a healthy personality but also for healthy relationships with yourself and others. Allport's six criteria are extremely relevant to how we connect with other human beings. He who is a non-egotistical person with an ability to warmly relate to others, accept himself for who he is, have a realistic perception of his environment, possess insight and humour and have a moralistic philosophy of life with a genuine desire to help others, will prosper in his relationships. Try to think of someone, past or present, who you believe to possess such a personality and then think of the relationships they had/have with others. Do you see how such a personality assists the person in relating well to others? Such people relate well to themselves and thus are also able to relate well to others.

To understand *how* we develop our personalities and create our life experiences, Albert Bandura's social cognitive theory has provided us with well tested hypotheses. The theory asserts that our personality results much more from what we learn than our genetic make-up. It also states that we learn through the observation of our own experiences *and* those of others and that we mentally interpret our environment and experiences. We use these to guide our future behaviours and are capable of altering our personalities based on what we learn. This is incredibly empowering as it suggests that we control our own lives and hold the ability to transform our relationships from undesirable to desirable. In other words, if you are in an unhappy relationship with yourself, your partner, your friend, sibling, colleague, boss, parent or child, you have the power to change it. You are not stuck in this personality that has brought you and your relationships to this point. You are free to change it.

Bandura's theory also features what he termed "reciprocal determinism", the idea that the person, the behaviour and the environment all affect one another. We thus function in the future based on what we learn as a result of the interaction of these three factors: the person (especially his thoughts), the environment, and the behaviours. Therefore, this social cognitive theory highlights that by affecting change in these factors we can affect change in the outcomes we obtain.

Over the years numerous studies have provided empirical support for Bandura's many theories, the most notorious of which is perhaps the Bobo doll study conducted by Bandura, Ross & Ross (1963). As a theory that has gained much credibility over the years, the social cognitive theory emphasises the role that our thoughts and behaviours have on our lives. We can, for that reason, change our negative experiences to positive ones by taking control of the influencing factors.

Bearing in mind that a healthy relationship with oneself is vital for other relationships to be healthy, either here, in a private journal or elsewhere, write one sentence to sum up the relationship you want to have with yourself **and** when by. If you are completely content as you are that is fine, just sum that up instead. If you think hard, there probably is some aspect of your relationship with yourself that you would like to change. For example, you might want to be in a place where you are not *quite* so self-critical when you make mistakes. Another example might be that you wish to be more self-assured and require less need for the approval, reassurance or permission of others. It may be that you once had these traits but events in your life knocked them out of you and you now want to regain them.

Your goal statement:

_____
_____
_____

Well done for doing that. One of the biggest steps you can take in life is establishing what you want to become and achieve. When you think of how many people spend their early adulthood confused and unsure of what career path they want to embark on, when you consider those that spend a lifetime doing a job they hate, when you remember those that reflect on their lives with "I always thought I would become a big success, but it didn't happen", you can see just how many people failed to make this one important step - truly defining what they wanted to achieve and become.

Without a doubt sometimes it can take many years to get this right. The important thing is not how quickly you get there so much as the fact that you get there in time before your time is over.

So, let's get on with moving you towards your goals.

Now that you've defined your goal for your relationship with yourself let's ensure it is an uplifting statement. Have you written your statement in negative terms or positive terms? How you write it will affect how you feel about it and how you feel about it will affect how you act upon it, thus changing the results you will achieve.

To demonstrate what I mean by this let us consider the following examples of negatively written goal statements:

> A. *By the time it's my 40th birthday I want to stop beating myself up over my past mistakes and I don't want to be self-loathing due to my fat body anymore.*
> B. *I want to stop being shy and stay home less by the 31th October 2012.*

C. I want to feel confident about my abilities as a teacher and not feel so overwhelmed by the difficult students in my class.

Can you see how these statements are worded negatively? Rather than being uplifting they would make you feel deflated, wouldn't they? Now see how they *feel* better when you say the *same* thing worded positively:

1. *By the time it's my 40th birthday I want to focus only on my future and I want to be happy with my body weight and shape.*
2. *I want to be confident and outgoing by the 31st October 2012.*
3. *I want to feel confident about my abilities as a teacher and feel in control and self-assured when dealing with the difficult students in my class.*

Which set of statements feel more uplifting and fuel a sense of excitement about achieving the said goals? The "A", "B", "C" statements or the "1", "2", "3" statements? It's the latter, isn't it? Yet, if you look, "A" and "1" say the same thing but in different ways, as do "B" and "2", as do "C" and "3".

Now re-write your goal statement with that in mind. Simply ask yourself what it is that you **do** want rather than what you **do not** want. If you find negative words in your statement replace them with their positive opposites, just as in statement "2" the word "shy" was replaced with "confident".

Your tweaked, positively worded goal statement:

_____

_____

_____

You will know in your heart and mind when you have written a goal statement that is positive and thus conducive to your achievement of it as it literally feels good.

Now repeat that statement aloud to yourself three times at a steady pace.

Fantastic! You've already made more progress than you may at this stage realise.

So *why* is it important that you look at your relationship with yourself? The way you relate to others is influenced by the way you relate to yourself. When you like yourself you will find it possible to like others. When you are a likeable person, others will also find it possible to like you too.

If you are dissatisfied with yourself you run the risk of being jealous of others which is completely counter-productive to having a successful relationship with them. Dissatisfaction and jealousy can lead to bitterness. Bitterness can lead to anger, aggression and depression. Therefore, it is vital that you like yourself if you want to have successful relationships with yourself and others.

There are some traits that attract people towards you and some traits that can repel people away from you. For example, being humble is one of the best attributes a person can have if they wish to have successful relationships. It is an attribute that people find endearing. It is something that parents can easily instil in their child. It is also a trait that some will adopt as a consequence of a profound experience.

Ever notice how insufferable one finds a person who is lacking in this arena, particularly if they themselves are not? Arrogance is unattractive. It becomes ever more so when it stems from self-delusion.

Integrating the trait of being humble into your personality is indeed something that will attract people towards you if you want to create successful relationships, personal or professional. However, this is not the main message I am conveying here.

You need to love yourself in a humble manner, before anyone else will love you. You need to accept yourself, including your flaws, before others will accept you. If you are not able to love yourself and accept yourself then you will be unable to love and accept others. How can you afford someone else the compassion that you are not able to give to yourself?

Dig deep to discover the necessary changes you need to make. Which aspects of Allport's six ingredients of a healthy, mature personality are you missing? Which personality traits, if any, do you have that repel people? Are you too needy, suffocating, negative, arrogant, selfish or self-involved? Do you lie, do you fail to honour your word, or do you betray people? What is it that you do not like about yourself? Where did those feelings come from? How can you assist a change in your perspective of yourself? Is it just self-acceptance that you need or do you need to change who you are in order to love yourself?

If you are brave enough you could ask the question of others who may be able to shed some light on your personality as they perceive you. Only ask someone who loves you dearly and that you can trust to be frank with you. When you receive the feedback you have requested ensure you act upon it accordingly if you agree that a change is necessary. One of two things will happen. You will either discover areas for improvement and change them for the better or learn that you are just fine the way you are and understand that you need to learn to accept and love yourself.

This type of self-love is *not* called arrogance, and it will pay dividends.

So that you can explore the real you, who you are and who you want to become, it is a good idea to begin a journal, i.e. a new notepad that you like the look of that has space for writing in frequently. It is worth writing your positively worded, uplifting goal statement in the journal. Do remember to date all of your entries. A journal is a great place to log any insights about yourself as you glean them from your day to day interactions with yourself and other human beings. Be sure to include any corresponding feelings. By reflecting on what you have written you will gain further knowledge of who you are deep down and how you feel about that person within.

In this journal you will also have space to perform the Action Points you shall find within this book. Alternatively use sheets of paper to perform the exercises.

Action Point -
Record your self-discovery and resulting journey as the process evolves, for example:

I have discovered that my increasing neediness since my divorce was becoming off-putting for my friends and this was making me feel unwanted...

I will now behave in a more self assured manner...

It's now three weeks on and I notice my friends are responding to me better with a better tone in their voice. I feel better about myself and...

It's now five weeks on and my friends have been so much more welcoming when I've gone round to see them than in recent months. This feels so great. I feel much more confident within myself...

This process of self-awareness is an ongoing one that should extend over your lifetime. You and your relationships will benefit from your understanding of who you are at your core. As you read this book you will understand more about yourself, how you became who you are and how you can change your relationships and life for the better.

Chapter 3

The Blueprint

"An individual's self-concept is the core of his personality. It affects every aspect of human behaviour: the ability to learn, the capacity to grow and change. A strong, positive self-image is the best preparation for success in life."

- Dr Joyce Brothers

What brought you to this station in your life? Which platform are you on? Where is the train going if no changes are made?

When you begin to understand *and* accept who you are and what you have become you will experience a sense of relief Stop fighting it, just recognise it.

Very often people will think they know themselves when they do not. What is interesting is that some beings will say, "This is who I am... this is how I think... these are my beliefs...", and yet they are carrying and projecting a reflection of traits, thoughts and beliefs that are untrue, contrived or unconsciously adopted from significant others or the media.

Who are you, really? How did you get here? Who and what made you into the person you are today and brought you to this point in your life? Whatever the answer, do not be filled with regret. You are exactly where you should be in life at this very moment in time. The sooner you acknowledge that the sooner the pain will begin to diminish and the fog will dissipate allowing you to clearly see your journey from where you are to where you want to be, and even the route to get you there.

When you try to answer this question in your mind or on paper you may come up with statements such as:

- *I believe a woman should be able to have a career as well as enjoy motherhood.*
- *I believe I am of average intelligence.*
- *I believe I would make a brilliant father.*
- *I believe God exists.*
- *I believe you can only have a handful of real friends.*
- *I believe I am only worth the level of wealth I accumulate.*
- *I believe that people are only nice to me when they want something.*
- *I believe my father did not love me as much as the other children.*
- *I believe I will be single for the rest of my life.*

Whatever statements of personal beliefs come to the forefront of your mind, think about why you believe these things. Do the beliefs belong to you? Do they come from the media, parents, teachers, friends, siblings, work colleagues, but not from you? On the other hand are they your very own beliefs that come from the inner workings of your own mind based on the interpretations you have made of what has happened in your life experience? Rightly or wrongly, they may be the figment of your interpretation. Your beliefs, whether adopted from others or created from interpretations you've made along life's path, may be damaging *or* assisting you and your life experiences. Either way, you adopted or created those beliefs and you hold the power to release and replace them.

If you were designing a new blueprint for your personality and beliefs, what would you include? How much of it is different from the package that you are today? You may not be as far off as you believe yourself to be and simply need a tweak here and there. Often, the smallest alteration can make the most profound difference. That's what makes this journey of yours so exciting.

When you live by principles and beliefs that have been forced upon you (by yourself or others) it stands to reason that you will make decisions in your life that are not congruent with whom you are at your core. In other words, you will embark upon careers, have relationships with people and spend your free time doing activities that don't make you feel as alive as you could, or as happy.

If, for example, you chose your job or career for the wrong reasons you would be discontented at work, a place you spend so much of your time. You could have chosen it due to pressure from your parents or partner and their expectations of you to work in a particular field. You could have chosen your line of work due to financial pressures; the job you do brings in the money you need but no joy or job satisfaction. Perhaps you chose your career because it fit the personality of the person you falsely believed yourself to be.

When you are dissatisfied with one such major aspect of your life it stands to reason that you will be unhappy in other aspects of your life. The knock-on effect such a dissatisfying weekly experience would have on your happiness and energy levels is immense but sometimes the effect doesn't present itself as such until it has become quite pronounced. A job that was incongruent with your true self would fail to ignite the passion within, you would find it corroding your self-esteem, your happiness, your energy levels, your relationships and your life in general.

It is not difficult to understand how dissatisfaction in one aspect of your life could and would create such discontentment in other aspects of your life. In this example the side effects of your experiences at work and the way you evaluated them would brush off onto other facets of your life and the way that you evaluated them too. Over time the consequences could be far reaching. Of course, you may be happy in your career but there may be other elements of your life that you need to address if they are not aligned with your true inner self.

It is now time to really listen to your inner voice. Let it guide you. Recognise the little voice in your head that says you believe something because you were told to but you are not convinced that you *really* believe it. Listen to the voice that tells you what makes you tick with excitement even though you may not have integrated it into your life thus far.

If you cannot be true to yourself, be who you really want to be, believe what you truthfully believe, will you ever be at complete peace within your own mind? Can you ever be truly happy believing and behaving in a way which others expect of you rather than as you truly desire? If you cannot be entirely happy and peaceful within your own mind then you *can* expect a knock-on effect on your relationships. You will gain a deeper insight into this as you progress through the book.

Action Point -

Write a *detailed* description of the person you want to be and the relationships you want to have with yourself and those important to you, i.e. the relationships you are intent on improving. Write out each ideal relationship separately and produce as much information as you can.

I'll give you some examples to set this in motion for you:

- *I want my wife to be welcoming when I come home from work.*
- *I want my wife to see me as her rock.*
- *I want my wife to understand that sometimes I don't feel like talking because I'm so tired from work.*
- *I want my wife to understand that I want to have some time to myself every now and again.*
- *I want myself and my wife to be able to communicate our feelings in a calm manner.*

- *I want my father to respect me.*
- *I want my father to recognise the achievements I have made.*
- *I want my father to forgive me for the mistakes I have made that hurt him greatly.*
- *I want to spend quality time with my father.*
- *I want to get to know aspects of my father that I have no knowledge of.*

- *I want to be decisive.*
- *I want people to respect me.*
- *I want to be trustworthy.*
    - *t to be the sort of person that attracts potential ?rs.*
    - *t to be unashamed of my background.*

When you first write your list do not worry about wording it positively to conform to the method that we spoke about earlier. The most important thing at this stage is that you jot down your true feelings without doing a mental edit as you outpour. Having committed your feelings to paper you can then re-write the sentences to read positively.

When you have written your desires as positively worded statements, write them in the present tense as if they have already been achieved, as if those states already exist. For example:

- *I want people to respect me* becomes *people respect me.*
- *I want my wife to be welcoming when I come home from work* becomes *my wife is welcoming when I come home from work* or better still *my wife is always welcoming when I come home from work.*
- *I want my father to recognise the achievements I have made* becomes *my father always recognises the achievements I have made.*

You ought to read these statements on a frequent basis to remind yourself of your goals.

Furthermore, these statements will be useful when you reach Chapter 18.

Chapter 4
Thoughts, Feelings And Behaviour

"Watch your thoughts, for they become words. Watch your words, for the become actions. Watch your actions, for they become habits. Watch your habits for they become character. Watch your character, for it becomes your destiny."

- Anonymous

Have you noticed how some people have a difficult childhood, one that lacks a loving, nurturing child-guardian relationship and yet they go on to have perfectly happy, successful, fulfilling life experiences? In contrast, others that experience a similar childhood go on to have an unpleasant life experience, often attributed to the results of their rearing. The same can be said of those who grow up in a loving, caring environment. This class too can have differing adulthoods. Several psychological theories have long attributed adulthood experiences to childhood experiences but upon looking at the evidence that is all around us can this always be sufficient to explain how some experience life?

Our childhood does affect how we view the world and how we manage our relationships but **we hold ultimate control and we use that to determine the course our life takes**. Negatively or positively you have brought yourself to this station in life. Negatively or positively you will move on from where you are to the next part of your journey. You may be thinking, but my partner/mother/boss controls my life, my finances control my life, my age controls my life, my being a single parent controls my life, my illness controls my life, my ethnicity controls my life, my negative childhood experience controls my life, my timidity controls my life. I assure you they do not and I will show you how to set yourself free of your self-imposed limiting shackles.

This next point is the most important tip for changing your relationships and life.

In a nutshell, **your thoughts determine your feelings, your feelings inform your behaviour, your behaviour determines the results you get and these results then feed your subsequent thoughts,** and so the cycle continues. These subsequent thoughts feed your feelings which then feed your behaviour, which then determine the results, which again feed your ensuing thoughts. On and on and on, the cycle goes on throughout your lifetime. Below is a simple diagram to help you visualise what this cycle looks like.

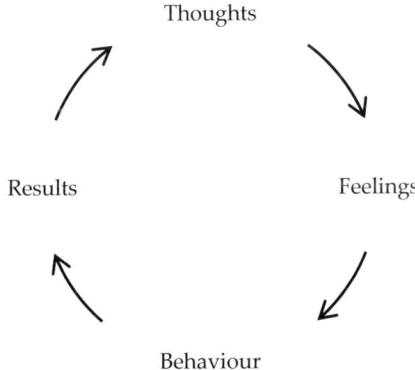

- Who controls this cycle? You do.
- How do you control this cycle? You control this cycle by controlling your thoughts.
- What are your thoughts? Thoughts are the meanings you attach to what happens. They are the interpretations you give to what you see and experience.

The *Cambridge Dictionaries Online* defines "thought" (derived from "think") as "to believe something or have an opinion or idea". If you look at its definition of "perspective", the noun of which is "thought", it states "a particular way of considering something".

Wikipedia's explanation is given as, "'Thought' generally refers to any mental or intellectual activity involving an individual's subjective consciousness."

Notice the use of "subjective consciousness" in the latter definition. In fact, all three definitions point towards this explanation, that thought is something subjective that happens within the mind of the individual. Therefore, if *you* are creating it *you* have the power to create different thoughts, thus altering the cycle.

Allow me to share an example with you. Watch out for the thoughts that underlie the protagonist's actions and how these impacted on the results received, or rather, created.

Example -
Jane found a shop unit for her new business and moved in as the pending new owner. The landlord at the time gave Jane permission to move her business into the property, before paperwork had been finalised, as she had expressed every intention of buying it.

During Jane's time in the business premises, which eventually lasted for approximately three months, she began to notice problems. One such issue was poor electric wiring resulting in intermittent lighting failures. As a result she instructed her solicitor to negotiate changes to the contract due to the problems that had arisen. The renegotiation related to repairs that were necessary before she would be willing to purchase the premises, a perfectly reasonable request. She was paying her hard earned money for something; she wanted it to be just right.

However, the sale of the property was now looking problematic and uncertain to the landlord. Furthermore, he was losing money as no purchase had been made and nor was he receiving any rent payments.

In Jane's position one might have decided that although payment of rent was never on the agenda, a goodwill gesture of paying some rent money until repairs had been completed would have been the honourable thing to do. After all the landlord was now simultaneously losing money, unable to offer the property for sale or rent to anyone else, and dealing with a "non-paying buyer" who was now changing the goal posts. Furthermore, Jane *was* currently using his business premises without paying for the privilege.

Underlying Jane's actions was her thought process which fed her feelings of superiority, control and greed. She believed that she was in control in this predicament. She thought she could dictate her terms to the owner by requesting what she wanted and then purchase the property once her demands had been met, or walk away having paid nothing (in terms of rent or bills) for occupying the property. In her mind she was in a win-win situation.

Had Jane's thought process been different she may have thought: I am renting these premises for free. I have now changed the goal posts. I should keep things respectful and amicable. I should offer him some rent money as I am currently running my business from here after all. I feel concerned that he could simply ask me to vacate the premises as he may not want to agree on the requested changes and prefer to sell the property on his own terms to someone else. This makes me feel unsettled and anxious as if that happened I would have no other premises to run my business from, and I have already spent a great deal of money on advertising material featuring this address.

Of course there are many different ways Jane could have thought and felt in this situation but you get the gist. If Jane had taken on different thought processes she would have felt differently about the situation and would have, therefore, behaved differently.

Her actual feelings of superiority, control and greed and the resulting arrogant and conceited behaviour stemmed from thoughts that had partially been fed by a life in a high powered career where she was extremely successful at negotiating with powerful business leaders. Jane felt that she could always get what she wanted with a little self-assuredness and arrogance.

The result? An unanticipated, abrupt end to negotiations coupled with an unexpected demand for Jane to rapidly vacate the property for good. Had she thought, felt and behaved differently the results would have been different. Even if that just meant that the landlord had given her a reasonable amount of time to leave, allowing her time to re-establish her business elsewhere.

Simply put, Jane's behaviour had a knock-on effect on her life and her business. When she eventually did buy another property it was not what she truly wanted. The location was not ideal for attracting her target market and she was not satisfied with its layout.

One can clearly see that Jane could have handled this relationship much better but the story also demonstrates how:

- Jane's **thoughts** (I think I can get whatever I want)
- that had been fed by **previous results** (one of which was a successful high-powered career),
- led to **feelings** (superiority, control and greed)
- which led to **behaviours** (demands and non-payment)
- that created **results** (unexpected loss of business premises and ultimately an undesirable new shop unit purchase).

The cycle of thoughts, feelings, behaviour and results will play out in all aspects of your life, including the relationships you have with yourself and others.

Example -------------------------------------
Amanda doesn't have many friends and she wants to improve her social life. She thinks she has few friends because she is shy and has low self-esteem (**thoughts**). She is invited to attend the wedding of an old family friend. When her mother introduces her to a very sociable lady she feels intimidated by her confidence (**feelings**). The two chat for a few moments and then part company. A little later in the day their paths cross again. When the pleasant lady asks if she would like to come and join her and a

couple of friends at their table she feels overwhelmed (**feelings**) and declines the invitation by making up an excuse (**behaviour**). Amanda spends the remainder of the wedding getting bored and returns home with the same lacking social life as before (**results**).

Amanda's self-belief (thought) that she is shy and has low self-esteem gives rise to feelings of intimidation when confronted by confident people. This feeds her feelings of insecurity resulting in feeling overwhelmed when presented with opportunities to improve her social life. As a result she avoids the situation, a behaviour that results in zero improvement in her social life.

Amanda is evaluating herself in a way that makes it much harder for her to change her behaviour which means she then keeps getting the same results. If she wants to change her results and thereby improve her confidence and social life then she needs to start by altering her thoughts which subsequently affect everything that follows. If she thought to herself, "I am quiet because I choose to be", then she changes the emphasis in her mind from shy and unconfident to consciously quiet. That slight shift then allows her to interact with confident people without associating their confidence with personal feelings of inferiority. Amanda can then see the other person's confidence as a part of who they are rather than something to fear and become intimidated by. The removal of that fear, which once came from feeling intimidated, then allows Amanda to better grasp new opportunities when she is not feeling fearful of them. This altered behaviour will create altered results. By grasping new opportunities rather than shying away from them she can move away from her lacking social life and towards her goal of a vibrant one.

There are so many examples I could give you but I imagine as you read this you are thinking of your own examples from your own life. If you haven't, take a moment to do so now, it is well worth it.

Do you appreciate the enormity of how this cognitive process can impact your life, and relationships, positively or negatively? You need to. Everything that happens begins with a thought. The only person in control of those thoughts is you. Therefore, you need to exert your control over them.

Don't let your thoughts control your life. Control your thoughts and you'll control your life. I'll repeat that. Control your thoughts and you will control your life.

All you need to do is think, feel, edit (as required) and continue:

- Think: are you thinking something that is negatively or positively impacting your life?
- Feel: to know the answer pay attention to how what you are thinking makes you feel.
- Edit: rephrase what you are thinking so that it is positively worded and conducive to your life and relationship goals.
- Continue: now you can ensure you are helping, not hurting, your life and relationships.

If you remember we looked at rephrasing your goal statement in Chapter 2 with that in mind. The instruction was, "Simply ask yourself what it is that you **do** want rather than what you **do not** want." Now you see that there was a bigger purpose to re-wording your goal statements. The words you use affect how you feel mentally *and* physically and how you feel affects how you behave - thus affecting your results. Some words and feelings affect you instantly and some after some time has elapsed. Often it is the cumulative effect of negative words and feelings that corrode your chances of happiness and achievement.

Stop jeopardising your own relationships with the way you evaluate your life. Use your thoughts to draw people near, not push them away. Don't tell yourself you are not worthy, you are. Don't tell yourself your important relationships are fraught with problems, concentrate on how you would rather they be. Don't sell yourself short, or anyone else, with your thinking.

Action Point ---------------------------------
Write down the three most negative things you think to yourself that you now realise are negatively affecting your behaviour and thus your relationships. They might be things you think about yourself or someone else.

You should feel proud of yourself for acknowledging these thoughts that are limiting your happiness.

Now, re-write your thoughts in a way that is positive and reflects your desired results for you and the relationship(s) you are looking to improve.

Even if you do not think the statement is true, if it is your ideal, write it down. In other words, if you think, how can I say she is always happy when we're together when I know she is always moody and that's why we're not getting on well together, don't worry. The point of the exercise is to begin thinking in terms of how you would like your relationships to be, not how they are right now.

Once you have written your statements of desirable thoughts repeat each one three times, twice a day, once first thing in the morning and once last thing at night. As you repeat them, think about what you are saying as you say each word at a steady pace. Don't maintain a negative internal dialogue. Instead, focus on the positive words and imagine that this is how your relationships are right now and imagine how good it would actually feel as if you were experiencing it right now.

Repeat the above process for every negative thought that you can identify that is limiting the success of your relationship(s).

Chapter 5

Release The Handcuffs

"You can make excuses or you can make progress but you can't make both."

- Anonymous

There is definitely an unequal footing when it comes to childhood experiences. Some of us have childhoods that provide us with a fabulous launch pad for our later life whilst others have distinctly difficult beginnings. Whilst how we are reared is largely, not entirely, out of our control how we handle the experiences then and later in life is determined by how we interpret what has happened. This is one thing that we do have absolute control over.

It is not easy, particularly the younger you are, to interpret things such as abuse as anything other than ghastly. It is utterly heartbreaking to think of the poor humans who experience unjust treatment when they are merely innocent children. What is amazing, though, is the resilience and mindset some children have. Some will grow older intent on creating a massive success of themselves, or having children of their own so that they may give them the life that they would have liked for themselves. We've all heard the saying "the abused becomes the abuser" but we only need to watch a documentary or read a book to learn about the abused who became the ultimate warm, giving, loving, caring person. Such people are examples of how we control how we respond to the events in our lives. We control how we move forward.

Many well known people like Stephen Hawking, Thomas Edison and Maya Angelou have gone on to lead massively successful lives despite their struggles and despite all the excuses they could have used to hold themselves back.

Allow me to share the story of someone's struggle that stemmed from an excuse that did hold them back.

Case Study ----------------------------------
As a child "Diane" often felt embarrassed and ashamed of her lack of stamina. Cross-country running, also known as long distance running, was always her least favourite aspect of physical education classes. She enjoyed other sports and was good at some but this was one sport she absolutely detested.

Her school used to insist that its students engage in this sport in the month of January which is always somewhat cold in Britain. The agony of the cold weather on extremities, the embarrassment of nearly every child overtaking her at the beginning of the race, the impossibility of catching up, and that shameful end where she had to "sprint" to ensure she was second to last rather than last is a memory she says she will never forget.

"What a loser I felt!" she recalls. That was the feeling she had created because of *her* interpretation of these poor performing events. She translated this repetitive experience as meaning she had terrible stamina and was ashamedly unfit. Consequently, she grew up engaging in zero stamina based sports.

As she reached her early twenties with a goal of losing weight, she decided to educate herself on how to run long distances, no excuses. What she discovered was that she was not by nature ridiculously unfit at all. She had simply never been taught by her physical education teacher that to run long distances took a certain technique, pacing oneself by running and breathing steadily. All that time she had thought she was incredibly unfit. All that time she had never improved her stamina because she had told herself that she was doomed by it and had convinced herself that this was something she would never be able to do. She had felt dejected and yet had never even tried. Diane reflected on her younger days and recognised that she had "used it as an excuse" to not put in the effort required to improve her fitness. She can happily state that she is now a very fit person who can run long distances much better and faster than she ever imagined possible.

Notice how Diane interpreted her teacher's ironic lack of teaching skills as her fitness level and used this as a reason to never improve her stamina. Only when she had the objective of slimming down to achieve her ideal body weight did she actually begin to **think differently** (about stamina and fitness); she finally recognised and released the excuse that was holding her back, and started looking for solutions.

Diane spent the best part of almost two decades feeling unfit and embarrassed for it. It doesn't matter if it takes you decades to come to a realisation that turns your life around. What is important is that you get there. Reading this book shows that you have already decided that you want to get there, that you want to take control of your relationship and turn it into how you would rather it to be. Now you too must **recognise and release any limiting excuses** so that you can achieve what you set out to achieve.

No matter how excruciatingly difficult the hurdles seem, making excuses will never get us over them, looking for solutions will.

It is a shame how people use their relationships, their illness, their background and their finances as excuses for not achieving what they want or worse still, as excuses for behaving badly with others. "I stole because I needed the money." "I am careless in my nurturing of my child because I missed out on affection from my mother." "I cannot achieve or create anything out of my life because I am completely bed-ridden." "I cannot..." Yes you can. Don't make excuses. Make progress!

Some will cling on to old excuses and habits because they fear change, others due to anger, and some due to laziness. Others will cling on to them because they allow them to blame something else for what *they* did wrong or for what they're not willing to do. Others cling on to them because they just don't realise they have a choice to change them.

Do you clutch on to old habits, excuses and memories as an excuse for not progressing? You have to be really honest with yourself. Sometimes it can feel easier to retain old habits, excuses and memories because it is what you have become accustomed to but if they are preventing you from having the relationships and life that you want then is it time to make a change?

If you constantly look to your past and dwell on the experiences that you have had and the things you did wrong or the things that have been done unto you, how will you move forward? Life is about saying to yourself and others that you will prove you are not a victim of your circumstances. Life is about learning from mistakes, not dwelling on them. Life is about making the most of what we do have to move towards a life of self-fulfilment.

People are far more impressed by someone who achieved any kind of success against all the odds than someone who is pitied for their life experience. Do you want to be remembered for what you achieved despite your hurdles *or* as someone who let the hurdles prevent his achievements? Whichever route you choose will alter how you feel about yourself. This in turn will affect the other aspects of your life that are affected by your self-evaluation and self-esteem, in particular, your relationships.

What you must always remember is that negative experiences bring about positive effects *if* you are focused on finding them. Your struggles build character. Difficulties can teach you how resilient you are or how hard working you are. They can create a fighting personality that enables you to go after what you want. The struggles can inspire you to not want to be a slave to your past experiences. Many, many positive by-products of negative experiences can be acknowledged if you are focused on finding them.

Most people can honestly say that there are people in far worse predicaments than themselves no matter how dire their own circumstances or life experience so far. It is also pertinent to remember that it is the reaching of rock bottom that will usually ignite that fire within you to say, "Enough is enough. I am going to do something about this. I am not willing to put up with this any longer. I will now do whatever it takes in order to improve my relationship/life/career/wealth/health/happiness." Use those feelings of despair to fuel your fighting spirit. Rather than dwell in the despair, taste it and then convert it into a roaring fire. That fire within will melt away your excuses, procrastination and fears, and propel you forward towards happiness.

Your relationships with yourself and others will improve when you release the excuses that are holding you back. You may not see them as excuses and you may feel that the word "excuse" is belittling the experiences you have had that may have been difficult. No one is saying that you have not been through tough times but if you *truly* want to move on from their imprisonment to achieve the relationships you desire then you will find a way to set yourself free.

Action Point -
On paper identify three excuses that act as restraints on the success of your important relationship(s). Then write solutions to help you overcome your perceived problems. Finally, act upon your solutions.

Repeat the above process until there are no more restraining excuses that you can identify.

Chapter 6

A Lesson Learned

"Learn from the past, set vivid, detailed goals for the future, and live in the only moment of time over which you have any control: now."

- Denis Waitley

Some will say that you mustn't look back at what has happened, yesterday is gone forever, look forwards and move on. Whilst I absolutely agree in looking and moving forward, a *glance* back can be useful from time to time.

Your past does not determine your future. The past has happened. It might be an indication of who you were and what you did but it does not determine who you are now and/or where you are going in your future, unless you *allow* it to or *want* it to.

Glancing back with hindsight is incredibly beneficial as it allows you to learn.

First of all you can learn about yourself. You can learn what you did right, what you did wrong, what you could have done better. Hindsight is a wonderful thing. When you are no longer emotionally attached to a now closed chapter of your life you can look more objectively at how successfully you played that chapter.

When you glance back you may be filled with regret about the way you have conducted yourself. If so, you needn't necessarily announce to anyone that secretly you are ashamed of how you've handled things or that you've made mistakes in your past. No speech is automatically required of your intention to move forward with amended thinking and behaviour. Sometimes all you need to do is just admit it to yourself and make the necessary changes.

In some circumstances, some will glance back and evaluate patterns in their relationships and become accustomed to them. They might have been in more than one abusive relationship in their lifetime and think that perhaps this is the yardstick to measure all relationships by and even that maybe this is what they deserve or that this is who they are. You are not defined by your past experiences. They teach you about yourself but they do not imprison you.

If you have previously decided to settle for a life that brings unhappiness, you have the power to change it so that your past does not dictate your future. You are who you choose to be from this moment on. You can create the relationships that you long for from this point forward.

Of course, it can at times feel easier to stay in an unsatisfactory situation than move forward towards something more deserving. Love has the ability to shroud a person's intellect. Immense love for any person can give you an obscured view of what is really going on. It can be easier to focus on the good times and black out the bad times or explain them away with justifications.

It can hurt immensely to have to face up to the fact that the person you love is not treating you well enough. It may be that your partner is letting you down somehow and, rather than acknowledge that they are doing so, you brush over what's happening with excuses. You may feel that they could work harder than they are to bring in a decent income or share the housework more equally or spend more quality time with you. **Either way, you condone what you are receiving in your life experience if you continue to receive it for a lengthy period of time.** Until you decide that you are not willing to accept it anymore you will continue down the same path.

Have you looked at your past and thought that this is who you are, that this is what you deserve or that this is the life you are meant to be living? What makes you think that? You need to answer these questions for yourself in order to move forward. Whether you believe you or the other party is creating the disharmony in your relationship, glance back at the relationship experience so far and ask yourself the following questions:

- How do you feel about the experience you are having?
- Has it always been this way?
- If not, what brought about the change?
- If it has always been this way, why do you continue to move down the same path if it is not bringing you complete happiness?
- Do you feel you deserve better?
- Does hindsight show you that you have perhaps endured too much for too long?
- Does glancing back help you to see which experiences have not been enjoyable so that you can understand what you *do* want for your future?
- How can you influence your current circumstances in order to create more positive experiences?

Case Study -

When "Joanne" was at university she suddenly met a fellow student named "Craig" who was also residing in the local area. Their feelings for one another were unexpectedly strong and, though they hadn't even become acquainted as friends before their first night of romance, there was something quite unusual about the experience. They felt extremely at ease together, although they were from quite different worlds.

Over the forthcoming weeks Craig and Joanne's relationship went from strength to strength within a very short space of time. They were extremely happy and relaxed within their relationship and became very close.

During their early days together Joanne never imagined that a horrible change would take place in their relationship and that she would go on to endure massive psychological abuse from Craig. Unfortunately the change crept in at first. As Joanne's feelings for him grew and she fell in love with him, Craig's possessiveness grew and he became mentally abusive and very controlling.

Initially, Craig indirectly forced Joanne to sever her friendships with her male friends. He later began quizzing her over any "suspicious" conduct. When she ventured out of the house she would frequently be seen by either Craig or by one of his friends who would then report back to him. She didn't even know what most of his friends looked like but they knew her and they knew whose girlfriend she was. Even when Craig was away in another city, hundreds of miles away, his friends would telephone him to inform him of any suspicious incidences they had witnessed involving his girlfriend. "I eventually felt as though my every move was being watched," Joanne recalled as she reflected on events that had occurred. "He was watching me and his friends were watching me."

Joanne lost a considerable amount of weight with the stress of her situation. She had fallen in love for the first time and he claimed to love her too; whilst the majority of the time they spent together was wonderful, the smaller proportion that was not so pleasant was so very awful that it became upsetting and depressing for Joanne. She felt controlled, bullied and distrusted and all she really wanted was the same happy relationship that they had shared before Craig's demeanour had changed.

Joanne knew she needed to end the relationship with Craig but she was so in love with him that she wasn't ready to let him go. She allowed him to continue mistreating her and, consequently, his behaviour gradually worsened. When the summer break began Joanne remained in the city in which they were studying to spend some time with Craig. She later grew suspicious that he had begun fooling around with other women and when his cruel behaviour deteriorated further she left to return to her home town.

She went to visit Craig once or twice, he continued to mistreat her and she became increasingly depressed. He completely broke her heart when he told her it was over as he had started dating someone else. Joanne, unable to let go through her depression, maintained contact with Craig for some time until the day came when she told him exactly everything she had wanted to say. She uttered her last thoughts to him, words that empowered her and gave her a sense of closure. As she spoke to Craig, all her love for him drained from her heart and mind. She astonished Craig with her words, regained the pride and dignity that she had longed for in the relationship, uttered her final words and hung up the phone. She smiled to herself and let out a sigh of relief. She knew her turmoil was nearly over.

The following year she became friends with a young man named "Joseph". Many months later they began dating and fell in love. They eventually married and believed that without a shadow of a doubt they would spend the rest of their lives together.

Joanne realised early on that, ironically, her husband-to-be was the complete opposite of the image she had carried in her mind of the type of person she would date let alone spend the rest of her life with. Furthermore, Craig had at the beginning been, in many ways, the image she had concocted of her ideal partner. Joanne now knew what she wanted so strongly by way of comparison that she became unwilling to settle for any less.

The contrast of being with someone who was macho and domineering helped her to see that whilst appealing at the beginning, she wanted a relationship that brought an equal balance of power. In years gone by she would have deemed Joseph's softer nature as weak and unattractive. Instead, due to the hardships she had endured with Craig, she recognised him as an ideal husband. As the old saying suggests, sometimes you have to experience the bad to fully appreciate the good.

Joanne had allowed Craig to control her relationships with other people. Years later she realised how this had massively perpetuated his possessive behaviour. She had essentially given Craig her consent to be dictated to. As a result, when she began dating Joseph she was very clear about the fact that she wanted to be with someone who would let her be herself; had Joseph not fit that criteria she would have readily ended her relationship with him.

The "old Joanne" had been a pushover, weak and easily dominated; the "new Joanne" was self-assured, strong and knew what she was no longer willing to tolerate. No matter how incredibly fond she was of Joseph, she recalled how she had zero qualms about ending their courtship in an instant if he did not satisfy her new standards for a desirable partner.

Welcome the positive and negative experiences of your life. They all serve a purpose. Experiencing what you do *not* want can sometimes be the best way to recognise what you *do* want. You can then use that information to create the relationships that you desire.

Learn from your life's lessons, what worked and what didn't. What you did right and wrong, what others did right and wrong. There's little point in repeating the same patterns in your relationships, whether with the same people or in new relationships.

As the story above suggests, those glances back to your past do help you move forward. The important thing is to ensure they are just glances. You don't wallow in self-pity when looking back. You don't view the old you as the current you. You don't use your past as an excuse for not moving forward. You should feel gratitude and pride that you have learnt and grown as an individual through your life experiences. Metaphorically speaking, you grasp the lessons you have learnt with both hands and put them to good use in your future.

Action Point ---------------------------------

What do you do that sends out the message that your current experience of the relationship(s) you want to fix is acceptable?

What can you do differently to let the other person know that your standards for your relationship have changed?

What lessons have you learnt from your past that have helped shape your future more positively?

What other lessons could you put to use now in the relationship(s) you have decided to work on?

Discuss the answers to these four questions in written format.

Act upon the insight you have gleaned so that you may better your relationship(s).

Chapter 7

Forgive

"To forgive is to set a prisoner free and discover that the prisoner was you."

- Lewis B. Smedes

Learning to forgive and forget someone when you have harboured negative feelings about them is easier said than done. The same can be said about your feelings towards yourself. Do you beat yourself up about the mistakes you've made or your poor performance? Do you have a record playing in your mind of what she did to you all those years ago? Do you feel vehement bitterness when you see images flash through your mind of seeing your partner with *her*? Do you feel anger at her for not treating you in the way you had expected?

The most important question is do you want to repair the relationship?

When you hold on to what has happened in a negative light there is no room for progress and growth of your relationship. If you keep looking back how can you move forward? You cannot enjoy your trip to Italy if you keep thinking back to your trip to France? There are new sights to be seen in your relationship, don't be blinded by your old memories and miss creating new ones.

Case Study -

"Bob" grew up in a home that was very happy, that is until his parents announced they would be divorcing. Over the following years the father and son had a troubled relationship. For some time it was a barely existent relationship. To go from happy families to a barely-there relationship with his father was incredibly difficult for the loving son to deal with.

The son struggled to comprehend how the seemingly happy couple came to the realisation that they were not meant to spend the rest of their lives together. He had always thought their family unit was completely solid. He was also hurt by the fact that his father had left his mother for another woman.

The son and his father eventually began working towards repairing their relationship and they now have a steadily growing bond. The work is by no means over but they are on the path to mending their hearts and relationship.

What is sad about their story is that they lost a great deal of time in their relationship that they will never get back. Time is the one thing you can never replace. Once it is gone, it is gone forever. Fortunately they realised what they were losing and now make a concerted effort to bond once again.

Do you think they would be able to mend their relationship if they were still focused on the past? If the son was still focused on how his dad left the family for another woman? How the dad had not cared enough to maintain good contact with him? No. That just creates anger and resentment. This is not to say that those emotions are not important emotions to be felt and that they have no place in the healing process of a damaged relationship. Indeed, they are *very* significant feelings and they do have a place in the process. Such feelings should be acknowledged but the key is how much time you give them.

First let us look at acknowledging the feelings. If you have an emotion, you should recognise it. It helps you to understand where your head is at, so to speak. When you understand what you are feeling:

- you know the starting point in the journey you need to take to get you from where you are to where you want to be;
- you know which emotions you are dealing with so that you can then deem whether or not they are necessary, appropriate and constructive;
- you understand how you would rather be feeling by way of contrast to your current emotions, i.e. your desired destination;
- you will establish a way to achieve what you *do* want to feel, e.g. happiness, contentment.

Secondly, how long is appropriate for your feelings to persist? Well, the answer will be different for different people and for different scenarios. What we can say is that when it stops you from moving on with your life for an extended period whilst simultaneously affecting your entire life negatively then it is no longer constructive. Being in a bad feeling place is not the offence, but rather, dwelling there without raising your head to look though the trees to see what else lies ahead on your path of life.

Remember we are not referring to grieving over the death of a loved one here. You have chosen to read this book because you want to improve one or more relationship in your life. If, for example, you are grieving over the breakdown of a relationship, e.g. your partner had an affair and you now wish to rekindle your marriage/partnership then you will need to move on towards your goal of a successful relationship within a reasonable amount of time. If you do not you risk drifting apart resulting in the relationship's demise. If you are looking to improve your relationship with yourself then you want to do it without in the meantime overly-damaging other aspects of your life, be they your career, family, social life, wealth, spirituality, personal development or health. In fact, no matter which relationship you are looking to improve, prolonged dwelling in a negative place for too long will invariably affect some or all of the aforementioned aspects of your life.

Imagine the ripples created by the throwing of a pebble into a lake. The pebble's landing point is similar to the original problem that you are focusing on. Meanwhile, the associated ripples working their way outwards are akin to the waves of effect that this negative focus creates on other aspects of your life. If you keep throwing pebbles you will keep experiencing the negative knock-on effects.

Negative feelings have a limited place in the *active* pursuit of achieving good feelings. Mull things over in your mind. Talk to get things off your chest. Write down the negative emotions you are feeling as part of the cathartic process. If necessary, confront the person who has wronged you and tell them how they have affected you and how you can recreate harmony together. However, once all is said and done, move on, for good. That means you don't torture yourself by mentally going over old stuff again and again as the weeks, months, years go by and you don't drag the other affected party through the mud again either.

Action Point -
On paper identify the relationship(s) within which you are still mulling over the hurt.

- Write about all of the pain you are feeling and why you are feeling it including *how it makes you feel about yourself* (e.g. I feel angry at myself) *and how it makes you perceive yourself* (e.g. I think I'm a pushover).
- Then write *how* this relationship will evolve to look like your ideal relationship, i.e. *how* you will move away from these issues and feelings.
- Write a date by which you want to achieve this improvement by.
- Implement the necessary changes required in order to achieve the above goal.

Chapter 8

Stuck Like Glue

"Work at growing together so you don't grow apart."

- Sam Owen

There is so much choice out there in the world today that we seem to be constantly being pulled towards something new. It might be the latest electrical gadget, the latest popular holiday destination, the new restaurant, the trend of the new fashion season, the latest holistic therapy, the new mode of transport, the new jobs and careers that never existed before or a new way of communicating remotely with fellow humans. The list goes on and on.

The rate at which the number of products on the market, new shows on TV and new technologies have advanced and multiplied is astounding. There has been massive growth over the past decade and it is a sign of things to come. Whilst advancement of society is great because it increases opportunities, the downside is it increases opportunities. Depends on how you look at it, doesn't it?

The opportunity for you and your partner to have the supermarket deliver your groceries to your home any day of the week whilst instead you spend that time saved watching a movie together is brilliant. Isn't it? The opportunity for you to sit at home with your family whilst all of you simultaneously explore the internet on your individual laptops is great. Or is it? What if the supermarket is one of the places that allow you and your partner to spend some quality time together as you walk the aisles chatting, laughing and generally connecting to one another? What about the laptops? Yes it is indeed amazing and convenient to be able to sit under one roof with several laptops running simultaneously at high speed on a wireless internet connection but where's the connection between their human operators?

You go to the shops and there are self-service checkouts, you can go anywhere with headphones attached to your mobile phone and watch or listen to almost anything via its internet connection, and you can buy and rent most things online. Where is all the person to person communication?

At this stage I would like to place my hands in the air (they are up, you just can't see them) and say emphatically that **I love technology** but I am aware of its potential to erode the quality of our interaction with one another. I must admit that I am *always* on my laptop. Are you? Are you getting sucked in by technology? If so, what is it doing to your relationships? Think about it. The example earlier of the trip to the supermarket being a portion of a couple's quality time together spent interacting person to person may have seemed silly. Is it though?

Let's say the average supermarket shopping trip takes just one and a half hours as the store is fairly close to where you live, you tend to go when it's moderately busy and you know the layout of the store. Let's say you go shopping once a fortnight on average. That's 39 hours of shopping trips a year. That's 39 hours of personal time with your partner per year where you get to connect, catch up and subconsciously remind yourselves of how alike you are or how well suited you are.

What if you spend 10 hours per week watching television with your significant other? Considering statistics often state an average of somewhere around 30 hours a week for the average British television viewer this is only about a third of the average. Bear in mind that these statistics fail to take into account the programmes and films we watch online and via DVD players, therefore, we are really only counting less than a third of all viewing as time spent viewing with a significant other. That is 10 hours a week, 52 weeks a year which equates to 520 hours per year that we spend focusing on the television screen rather than each other. You may perceive it to be quality time with your partner. Whilst it is time with your partner is it *quality* time together?

What about the time you spend on your computer or laptop surfing the internet, reading articles, watching funny video clips, shopping for clothes, reading reviews, posting comments on social networking sites and so on? Let's say that you spend just seven hours of time per week on your computer or laptop that prior to the internet revolution you might have spent interacting with your partner. Fifty-two weeks a year multiplied by seven hours equates to 364 hours per year spent focusing on your computer or laptop screen rather than each other.

Combine 39 hours and 520 hours and 364 hours and that's alarmingly 923 hours per year which is 17.75 hours *per week* that you are missing out on potential quality time with your beloved. That's a big loss for your interpersonal relationships and yet these figures are actually quite modest. Plus, as time goes by the lack of human to human communication increases as we form new habits in a technologically advancing world. Therefore, we are likely to affect how much quality time we spend socialising, more and more as time goes on. That's a lot of time spent on lonesome activities, time that was once spent, quite naturally, interacting with each other. Whilst the examples used refer to a romantic couple the same can be said of any important relationship, especially where those concerned live under the same roof.

As this is now the world we live in we simply need to be realistically aware of the quality and quantity of our interactions with others. This requires being more aware of the choices we make and being realistic about how much quality they bring to our relationships. By purposefully creating awareness of the fact we can then ensure we compensate for it. That might mean ensuring you go out for a meal every so often or having a "date night" at home whereby you have a meal around the dinner table, dress up, and maybe light some candles. You can make it a priority to take advantage of the sunny days by strolling in the park. You can enjoy activities together that you may only do every now and again such as crazy golf, indoor rock climbing, theme parks, ten pin bowling, water parks, and so on. It doesn't have to cost money so whilst one option is taking a holiday together another option might be sitting in your garden together, without distractions.

One incredibly fantastic way of connecting with those you want to build solidarity with is taking a walk together whilst you talk. Come sunshine or snow, this can be as simple as walking around the local area. As you will normally be absorbed by the conversations taking place, the surroundings themselves aren't as significant as you might expect them to be. Therefore, you can often rework the same route several times during your walk without really tiring of the scenery as your focus will be on the fun you are sharing and the conversations you are having. As you walk the endorphins released by your brain will give you a natural high. This natural high will infuse this simple activity with a general sense of good feeling which you will then also associate with the person accompanying you. They too will associate this good feeling with you. The removal of any usual distractions you might face at home (in their house or yours) also benefits the cohesion of your relationship massively.

We all need to bear in mind that people are free to make numerous choices now, many of them resulting in time spent unaccompanied. If you need to strengthen a relationship you must proactively give your undivided attention to the other person and ensure it is reciprocated.

When you love someone you want them in your life forever, right? Right. Will they stay there by default? No! You have to work at it. You can grow together or you can grow apart - it just takes love and a conscious commitment to keep it together. If you both care enough, you *will* work at growing together, and you'll stick like glue.

Action Point ----------------------------------
Write a list of five new things you can do to increase your interpersonal interaction and communication with those you want to improve your relationship with, for example:

Walk the dog together in the evenings.

You should also write a list of current activities which you can tweak the quality of to make them more communicative, for example:

Turn the television off when eating dinner together.

Write a statement that promises a new commitment you will make for the sake of helping or even saving your relationship(s), for example:

I commit to spending three hours each week with my wife where the two of us enjoy an activity together that consists of communication and/or playfulness with one another.

Act upon your proposed insightful changes.

Repeat the above process until you have exhausted all the possibilities for improving the quality and quantity of time spent together.

Chapter 9

The Fence Is Too High

"Winners compare their achievements with their goals, while losers compare their achievements with those of other people."

- Nido Qubein

When you have a relationship with someone, be it a parent, a child, a partner, friend or sibling, how you *experience* that relationship is only truly understood by you and that person. This is why people who try to give advice or "help" will usually be met with reluctance. The experience you have is built upon how you have interpreted previous relationships in your life and how you perceive yourself, which again you glean from your interactions with other people. When others come along and try to advise you they are unable to fully grasp why you feel and behave the way you do. After all, they have not been involved in the processes that have taken place within your mind as you have experienced life and formed your interpretation of it. Instead, they have been involved in the processes that have taken place within *their* mind as they have experienced *their* life and formed *their* interpretation of it. You may have opinions regarding their situation and they may have opinions about yours but the bottom line is we usually don't want to hear the opinions of others. No matter how well intended the opinionated comments may be they will usually fall on unenthusiastic ears.

Think about how you have reacted to the opinions and answers to problems that others have tried to give you in the past. Whilst some of it can be sound advice, some of it can anger and frustrate you, can't it?

There are, on the other hand, definite plus points to comparing notes with others so long as you remember that you do not have the whole picture of their situation and nor do they of yours. An example of this is "chick-flicks", films aimed at women that revolve around a character or number of characters that are women. Such depictions can often be heart-warming as they allow women to compare their world to that of others in the same situation, or simply, of the same gender. Men too have their jokes and male humour whereby they refer to the experiences that are familiar to males and thus unite them with this common ground. In fact, this unification can assist men and women to feel understood, that they are not alone, and that "x", "y", "z" is the norm.

It can be extremely comforting to learn that others also find that their partner lacks the initiative to clean the house without being asked to or that their partner also drives terribly, or leaves clothes on the floor, or forgets to buy milk on the way home. Whatever it may be, it can be reassuring to know that others are having the same experience in their personal or business relationships too, be they parent-child relationships, friendships, work colleagues or whatever. Discovering this type of information can create a more relaxed attitude towards issues that may otherwise have been eating you up inside. One can get carried away with thoughts of self-pity or anger as one analyses certain occurrences. That dose of shared experience, particularly if the other person is being blasé about a similar incident, can reassure a person that it is not unusual and indicate the need for a shift in perspective.

As with anything else, once a person adapts their perspective on a situation they will adjust their feelings about it and, subsequently, their behaviour in response to it.

Example -----------------------------------
Let's take the example of two people co-habiting together, for example, two partners. Each relationship brings a different dynamic. In this case the two partners have an adult-adult relationship. We'll say this is a heterosexual relationship and call the partners Jim and Joyce.

Jim had a tendency to leave his clothes on the floor after wearing them. The rightful place was either the laundry basket if they needed a wash or the wardrobe if they could be worn again. Day after day Jim added more garments to the increasingly large pile on the floor. Joyce on the other hand has always cleaned up after herself in all aspects of her life.

Joyce began to get frustrated and angry at Jim. She saw his behaviour as rude and unnecessary. In particular, Joyce found Jim's actions disrespectful towards her as Jim was fully aware of how much his pile of clothes bothered her for she mentioned it repeatedly every week. As the issue persisted she began to view other incidences as indications of his lack of respect for her. It might have been the cups by the side of the bed that he never brought down to the kitchen unless asked to or the messy state he would leave the car in.

Each time one of these episodes took place another layer of anger and bitterness enveloped Joyce's mental interpretation of Jim's actions. One day the anger had reached its peak and an argument erupted. Joyce had no real reason for arguing with Jim other than, as she saw it, her feelings surrounding the lazy, selfish behaviour he displayed again and again. Jim was a little bewildered by the whole thing, unsure of what he had done to invite such an outburst. They argued, Joyce told Jim she was sick of cleaning up after him, Jim apologised and they made up.

As Joyce in her moment of immense anger had not really explain herself properly, Jim apologised but never fully realised just how much this issue was bothering Joyce and so the cycle continued. Jim continued to leave his clothes in a pile on the floor, leave dishes by his bedside and so on. The couple went on to have three more arguments over the following months, about the same issue, although Joyce then began to argue with Jim regarding other matters too. Each time they argued, the problem remained unresolved, Jim's behaviour did not change drastically and they began to bicker every day over all sorts of things, big and small.

The reason for the constant arguments was that Joyce had started to interpret every little thing Jim did that made her unhappy as a sign of disregard for her feelings and a lack of respect for her. The tense situation and regular bickering began feeding Jim's attitude towards the disharmony in the relationship. He interpreted their relationship as having hit a rocky road and he found it difficult to communicate with Joyce. He became irritated with Joyce and sometimes wondered to himself, what is her problem?

One day whilst Joyce was socialising with some female friends one friend mentioned that her partner always left his clothes on the floor, strewn over the back of chairs and hanging on the bathroom radiator even though they just needed to be placed in the laundry bin. Upon hearing her friend tell the story two things struck her. Firstly, the story was incredibly similar to her experience of Jim's behaviour at home. Secondly, her friend seemed rather relaxed and blasé about the whole situation. As they talked further, swapping stories about their similar experiences Joyce felt a sense of relief wash over her.

Sometimes there is no better remedy than swapping stories of a similar experience with someone and feeling that you are not alone in your experience. This is why people join things like a single parents club, for example, or any other club where there is a common experience underlying the meetings.

Joyce returned home after her night out with an altered viewpoint and renewed energy for the tense situation at home. Her friend's stories helped her realise that perhaps she had been taking Jim's inability to clean up after himself too personally when in actual fact he was just being lazy and/or thoughtless. Now in actual fact Joyce may have been right in her thinking all along and, instead, her friend could be considered a pushover. One might say the friend was also being treated with disregard and disrespect, just as Joyce had been feeling about Jim's actions towards her. However, the fact is, regardless of what was underlying the occurrences, the interpretation is the influencer in the relationship. How an occurrence is interpreted will affect how it is acted upon which will feed the relationship in either a healthy or unhealthy way. Furthermore, hearing someone else talk of a similar experience helped Joyce to alleviate some of the anger building up within which helped clear her mind of self-pity and bitterness. Instead, Joyce would be better able to look for solutions to resolve the issue as the manner in which she had handled the situation so far had not been effective. As a result, Joyce was able to confront Jim in a way that communicated how she felt about his refusal to clean up after himself, how this was affecting their relationship and how a little conscientious effort on his part would be greatly appreciated. Jim then understood her clearly and said he would make the changes requested. Jim still had plenty of moments where he fell into old bad habits but rather than have a massive argument, Joyce would approach Jim in a relaxed way and simply remind him of their conversation.

Each time Joyce successfully communicated to Jim that his bad habit had seeped through again and she subsequently achieved the desired result of Jim cleaning up after himself, the experience fed Joyce's thought process positively. She analysed each of these occurrences as proof that he did care for her and her feelings and did respect her. They also increased her self-confidence about her ability to relate to others. Just like before, each time one of these episodes occurred another layer of feelings was added to Joyce's mental interpretation of Jim's actions, only now the analyses and subsequent emotions were positive. This positive cycle of thoughts, feelings, behaviour and results spilled through to the rest of their relationship and assisted in making it increasingly stronger over time. A similar change took place for Jim and so he too began to feed the relationship positively instead of negatively. In the case of Joyce and Jim this shift from a negative cycle to a positive one began with a simple comparison of notes between two people in a similar situation.

The above example demonstrates how one can positively use comparisons with others' relationships that are similar to one's own (e.g. parent-child, husband-wife, two friends, boss-employee) as a way to re-evaluate one's own situation. By doing so one's thinking can be altered affecting one's emotions and thus the subsequent behaviour and results. This can form an invaluable learning strategy. It is always important to remember that one's own common sense be applied when using such a strategy. If someone shares an experience and leads you to believe it is okay, such as a child hitting his parent, it needs to be remembered that such behaviour is simply not acceptable regardless of how the other party may be portraying the story.

The danger with comparing your relationships to other similar relationships (e.g. parent-child, husband-wife, two friends, boss-employee) is that it can also bring unnecessary stress, pain and disappointment about one's own relationship. Many people often project the image of their family life, their marriage, their work life, and their friendships as rosier than they are. When we catch a snapshot of that portrayal it can appear wonderfully happy and peaceful. What goes on behind closed doors, we do not really know for sure.

It can be easy for a daughter to turn to her mother and say something like, "Mum, why don't you give me a hug when you leave like Aunt Mary does with Melissa?"

We watch other couples and turn to our own partners saying things like, "Brian is such a gentleman, he always treats his wife like a lady, opening doors for her, carrying all her shopping bags for her..."

Is it really fair though when such comparisons can make you perceive the person in your life to be a lesser parent, for example? After all, just because "Aunt Mary" hugs her daughter when she leaves does not mean that she is any better as a mother or has more of a loving relationship with her children than a mother who does not hug upon departure.

If one compares to others based on what one is *shown* by others then this can produce negative feelings. This can then feed other thoughts about other aspects of the relationship that one is comparing with others. As time goes on a negative perception can become an increasing focus in the mind of the interpreter. Whether others are putting on a display of unity or sickly sweet love in front of you but fighting constantly behind closed doors is questionable. So rather than question your own relationships based on your observations of others' relationships make sure you remember that the grass is not always greener on the other side and that things may not be as they seem. Don't feed negative thoughts into your mental cycles about your relationships when you have no real evidence that what you are seeing elsewhere is real. For all you know "Brian" may be acting like a gentleman in front of others but he may never do it when others are not present.

Judge each relationship on its own merits. Whilst others' relationship anecdotes can be comforting and can assist you in dealing with conflict within your own relationships always remember that you simply do not have the whole picture and things aren't always as they seem. Comparing with others can be helpful *and* it can create false assumptions. You will never know the truth about what goes on in another relationship behind closed doors, whether husband and wife or mother and daughter or whatever their relationship. Even the individuals concerned only know their own subjective perception of their relationship.

A dose of common sense must always be applied when comparing with others. Utilise these comparisons to your advantage, not disadvantage.

Action Point -
Think about each relationship that you are looking to improve.

- Have you made comparisons with the relationships of other people you know?
- Have these comparisons served your relationship well?
- Have these comparisons ever negatively affected your relationship?

Think hard about this. You may need to dig deep into your memories to answer the above questions truthfully.

If you have negatively affected your relationship with comparisons:

- How could you better evaluate your experiences now?
- Does this new evaluation help you to move your relationship in a positive direction?

Remember, you are looking for solutions to improve your relationship(s). Answer the above with that in mind.

Write your thoughts down on paper and implement your amended thinking into your relationship(s).

Chapter 10
That's What You Said But...

"As I grow older I pay less attention to what men say. I just watch what they do."

- Andrew Carnegie

One of the most important things to remember when in any form of relationship is that actions speak louder than words. You can *say* anything. All it takes is breath. What you *do,* on the other hand, takes effort.

Many people think that by talking the talk they are convincing others but they are only fooling themselves. The most that might happen is they might convince others that what they are saying is true but if they then fail to follow through it eventually becomes very apparent to the other party. Furthermore, they gradually lose all credibility and, thereafter, the comments they make will hold very little value. People won't take them seriously, they won't believe them, and most importantly, they won't trust them. Over time this mistrust will eat away at the relationships they have or if they are trying to build a new relationship they will barely get far from the starting line. They could have many other great qualities but if they cannot be trusted, they will struggle in relationships and in life.

If, for example, there is an only child in a single parent family the child will rely heavily on his parent for love, attention, boundaries and safety, reassurance, recognition and life skills. Unfortunately, some single parents can become very accustomed to utilising family, friends and childminders to care for their child in order to alleviate some of the pressure on themselves as single parents. Whilst the need for help from others is wholly understandable, the disadvantage is that the child can begin to feel increasingly insecure if the parent does not compensate for such behaviour.

If the child is told "I love you" and "I love spending time with you" yet finds he is frequently left in the care of others and finds his parent generally unwilling to spend quality time with him, will he remember his parent's words or his actions? One can see how such a child may begin to miss his parent, begin to feel disconnected from his parent, and possibly feel abandoned and unloved too.

Imagine this child frequently finds himself in upsetting situations without his parent nearby as he is usually in the care of others. Without the parent there to nurture him, what sort of knock-on effect might this have on his feelings of loneliness and abandonment?

What if the child is lonely and struggling to make friends? Imagine his parent told him that he appreciates how difficult this might be for him. If he then failed to make any real attempts at helping his child make friends with other children, what message would this action convey to the child? Would he see his parent's inaction as a sign of his lack of concern regarding the matter?

How might this parent-child relationship become affected? How do you suppose such a child will begin feeling over time? How do you suppose he will begin behaving towards his parent and others? Is it possible that he will become insecure, lonely and miserable? Is it possible that he may begin to display moody and aggressive behaviour and become quite temperamental? Might he become ambivalent towards the parent and become disobedient?

If a parent needs to engage the help of childminders on a frequent basis, this does not mean that the child needs to grow up feeling unloved and uncared for and insecure. It simply requires that the parent demonstrate with his actions that he does sincerely love the child and is willing to be a parent when they *are* together. For example, a child will understand his parent's need to go out to work for long hours, if the parent successfully incorporates his parental duties during the limited time they do have together. The actions will speak louder than empty words, even if the actions can only be demonstrated for much fewer hours than other parents can afford.

A lack of one parent should not be used as a scapegoat for one's own missteps. Plenty of children grow up in single-parent families feeling loved, happy and stable. The power lies within the hands of the child's present parent and depends on how successfully they are able to manage the relationship. Those that have successfully parented their children single-handedly will agree. Those that have not will either be furious about this statement or embrace it.

It doesn't entirely matter what you say to someone, it is what you do or fail to do that speaks volumes, even to a very young child. Children are perceptive. Their ability to pick up on emotions and feelings and messages being emitted by others should not be underestimated. It does not matter how much a parent may look to others to fill a void that he has created in the parent-child relationship, the only person who can truly fill that hole in the child's life is the parent himself. He who creates the void is he who needs to fill it.

Taking this one step further now, when someone is being told that there will be consequences to certain actions, they know where they stand. This may be a child being told he will lose the privilege of watching television for a week if he continues to hit his brother or a partner being told that another adulterous affair will spell the end of their relationship. No matter the age, boundaries create stability and awareness of what is and is not acceptable. Now if the person in question does not adhere to the rules and yet he neither suffers retribution, then the relationship begins to unravel. This can lead to frustration, confusion and a lack of respect for the person that does not follow through on serving the consequences. In other words, all talk and no action, contributes to relationship instability and breakdown.

If a child has continued to hit his brother despite being advised of the consequences and then discovers that the parent is not punishing him in the way promised, what does that tell the child? It says that the parent doesn't care enough about the aggressing child and his behaviour to proactively control it. It also means the child does not learn right from wrong, acceptable from unacceptable. This will damage the child's ability to relate to others in a positive way as he will not have learnt what is acceptable and what is not. He will struggle to socialise on his own. He will feel unaware of what he can and cannot do in social situations and as a child who is still learning about the world it means he will feel insecure within himself. If the child is not being taught valuable life lessons he will have to endure negative experiences in order to learn. This can become a harrowing childhood experience.

A child will learn by seeing his parents fulfil their promise of acting upon what they have said, whether it be a punishment for misbehaviour or a reward for good behaviour. Without their instructions, direction and words backed with actions he will have unnecessary negative experiences, feel angry at his parents and feel unstable and uncared for. The parents too may feel angry at the child but they are the responsible party as he is only a child.

Adult-to-adult relationships work in a similar way. These rules still apply to adult relationships although in this case both parties equally share the responsibility for the relationship's success. To demonstrate let us take the example of a married couple beginning to drift apart after the husband's extra-marital affair.

Example -
Jake and Julie talk about making an effort to spend every Saturday night doing something special together in an attempt to bond together again after their relationship has hit troubled waters. They recognise that they used to spend more of their time together. Times they spent laughing, kissing, cuddling.

When Jake does not bother sticking to this new plan Julie is hurt and upset by his apparent indifference towards her and upset that he has not honoured their new commitment. Julie does not share her feelings with Jake and does not bring this broken promise to his attention. Instead, she alters her plans for her now free Saturday night.

Jake begins to repeat this behaviour every now and again and without ever questioning or discussing her feelings with him Julie simply rearranges these freed up Saturday nights. This action in itself tells Julie that Jake does not respect her or care about their relationship enough. It tells Jake that she does not care about the relationship enough either as she is not challenging him about the issue. Even timid people will fight to save something they truly care for.

Julie has also requested that Jake tidy up after his friends have visited because she likes to come home to a clean house. When he does not adhere to this request, again, without discussing it Julie continues to clean up after Jake and his friends. By doing so she is inadvertently telling Jake that it is okay to disregard her feelings and requests. With this response Jake feels he can continue misbehaving in this way. One day, Julie feels absolutely fed up of Jake's behaviour with regards to the messy house and the frequent changing of their Saturday night commitment. She is feeling incredibly hurt over his lack of respect and consideration for her. This time instead of cleaning up after him or discussing how she feels, she becomes irate and smashes his laptop on the floor causing him to lose important information. Jake is confused and angry as she has not previously bothered to challenge him about his poor behaviour and its effect on their relationship. Julie has thus far given him the message that he can continue as he is whilst she continues cleaning up after him as well as allowing him to neglect their Saturday "date nights". When she does eventually reach the end of her tether her pent up anger within is unbeknown to Jake; when it erupts with the smashing of his property he feels angry and shocked as he has not had any forewarnings of such consequences.

Rather than Jake recognising what he has done wrong he blames Julie for their relationship problems and feels that he does not know where he stands with her. Unfortunately, in the meantime he has also lost some respect for her as she has allowed him to disregard her and her requests without any fear of reprisal. Consequently, the relationship breaks down further than it already had purely because rules have not been respected and consequences for misbehaviour have not been served. All talk and no action has resulted in a slippery path for their relationship.

Jake goes on to have a second extra-marital affair even though Julie had forewarned him that she would leave him if he did so. He still does so as he has now lost further respect for her and their relationship and does not easily fear reprisal, as Julie rarely follows through on her threats. He does not feel good about himself for having the second affair but he does not fear losing Julie as a consequence. When she finds out, she doesn't end the relationship as she had previously threatened to, however, Jake does end the second affair. When Jake begins a third affair he absolutely does not expect to lose Julie and he does not want to lose her, despite how he behaves. Julie eventually finds out.

One day Jake comes home to a house void of any signs that Julie lives there. The contents of her wardrobe are gone, the pictures of them together are gone and she is nowhere to be found. Jake sits on the edge of their bed with his head in his hands. He has a lump in his throat and his eyes begin to well up. He is distraught and angry with his wife as well as himself. He is angry with Julie for being so erratic with her actions that he never quite knew his boundaries. He is angry that she lacked self-respect and never stood up for herself which contributed to him treating her as he did. He is angry at himself for mistreating Julie and for pushing their relationship to its end.

Over-simplistic, yes, but this example does identify some key points about relationships.

Without absolving him of his responsibilities, if Julie had backed her words with actions and if she had demonstrated respect for herself, Jake would have respected her more. He also would have respected her threats and her boundaries more. They would have had a more robust and respectful relationship as a result. They would have had a better chance at making their marriage last.

It is all very well saying it is someone else's fault but what messages do you give out to the people you come into contact with? Your action *and* inaction speaks volumes. **Words only carry meaning up to a certain point. It is then the action, or lack thereof, that carries your words forward into significance or insignificance.**

There are some actions that speak louder than others. The actions do not even need to be profound. It is the underlying message that each action conveys that is of importance, not how large a gesture it is. There are some very simple acts that create a massive bond when they are persistently and consistently repeated over time. Allow me to share some experiences from my own life to demonstrate the power of basic actions.

When it comes to the parent-child relationship I can tell you that I have a most wonderful mother but you may be surprised to learn that as a mother of five children, in some ways, she has never been maternal. Even now with three grandchildren she struggles to be particularly affectionate. I, along with her four other children, have had very few hugs from her. She rarely says "I love you" and she will usually make light of any affection we show her that lasts over three seconds. However, we have never once felt that our mother doesn't love us because ever since we were young she has shown with her actions that she loves us *very* much and cares for us deeply regardless of whether she voices it. She may not be the hugging, molly coddling, kissing, constantly praising type but she has always ensured we were fed, cleaned, bathed, clothed, cuddled when necessary, mentally and physically nurtured and tended to, no matter the day of the week or the time of day or night.

Before I moved out of the parental home she would be as willing to cook something fresh for me at 3am upon my return home from a night out just because I might be hungry as she would be if I were extremely ill. She ensured that I had what I needed, whether food, clothes or psychological support, that she made an effort with my important friends, that she showed an interest in me and my life. Even now, she would still do all of the above in an instant, despite being older and more susceptible to fatigue.

It matters not that sometimes I have to strategically zoom my head in at a precise angle just to plant a kiss on her cheek before she hurriedly moves away looking uncomfortable. It matters not that she rarely compliments me or says, "I love you". Her actions speak much louder than any words could.

When it comes to actions that demonstrate one's love for another, whilst there are some basics that are true for all successful relationships, one size does not fit all. Within each relationship there are words and actions that demonstrate the love one has for another and these will be different for each relationship. No two relationships are the same.

On the morning of my brother's wedding we agreed to first meet at my parents' house. As I arrived and my mother noted my appearance, her eyes widened and sparkled and her face was brimming with a smile. However, instead of saying "you look nice", she cracked a joke about my outfit. I knew that although her words hadn't told me she thought I looked nice her actions did, i.e. her sparkling eyes and smiling face. Actions *always* speak louder than words, even if they are masked under words stating otherwise.

Action Point --------------------------------
What messages are you giving to the people in your successful and unsuccessful relationships?

Split a clean sheet of paper down the middle. On the left hand side write the heading *Things I Verbally Say But I Don't Backup With Action* and on the right hand side insert the heading *How To Improve*.

For the relationship(s) you would like to improve write a list in the left hand column of the things you say, claim, protest for but don't back up with the corresponding action. Leave several lines in between each point. Then in the right hand column write about how you can improve on the highlighted inconsistency between your words and actions so that you can begin doing what you are saying and you can become who you verbally claim to be.

This might be for your relationship with yourself and so you might write:

I tell myself I am generous with money but then I am very stingy with charities.

An improvement method you might write in the right hand column could be:

I will set up a direct debit for £5 per month for the Red Cross charity by Wed 20th June 2012.

If you are trying to improve your relationship with your friend(s) you might write:

I say, "We can go out to the cinema if you want," but when we get there I make it known with my demeanour that I do not want to be there.

An improvement method you might write in the right hand column could be:

I will only say this when I mean it.

Be sure to take action on your proposed changes.

Chapter 11

Your Hands Are Shouting At Me!

"Effective communication is 20% what you know and 80% how you feel about what you know."

- Jim Rohn

We've all heard the statistics several times before, that body language accounts for more than fifty percent of our communication. It is fair to say that both verbal and non-verbal communication impact on the success of our relationships.

For a start, if you want to communicate sincerely then your verbal and non-verbal communications have to be congruent with one another. In other words, you cannot growl "I love you" whilst standing arms crossed and eyes rolling. Inversely, you cannot stand with arms open as if inviting a hug as the words "I'm finding you insufferable lately" leave your lips. Well you can do all of the above if you are merely indulging in a spot of humorous sarcasm but if you are not saying or doing any of the above in jest then the mixed message will leave the recipient feeling unsure of where you both stand.

Spencer Kelly (2006), Associate Professor of Psychology at Colgate University, measured peaks and valleys in the brain waves of participants to understand whether body language that is inconsistent with the accompanying verbal communication is picked up by the brain.

To test the way the brain processes verbal and non-verbal communication, brain waves were monitored with the use of an electroencephalograph.

Kelly found that if a participant had to process a sentence with an inappropriate word such as, "He spread his toast with socks", the brain waves would create a valley (a downward dip) on the graph as a result. The dip was classified as N400 in measurement. The researcher found that if a speaker's gestures and verbal communication were incongruent (inconsistent with one another) then the same size valley of N400 was produced by the brain waves. For example, if the speaker uttered a word such as "tall" but at the same time conveyed "short" with his gestures (non-verbal communication), then the participant's brain would pick up on the inconsistency between the verbal and non-verbal communication. This was demonstrated by the same size valley recorded by the electroencephalograph.

Therefore, the study indicates that the brain processes verbal and non-verbal communication simultaneously and *does* notice, albeit sometimes on a subconscious level, when there is a mismatch between the spoken word and the body language accompanying it.

Case Study -----------------------------------
"Lucy" was a likeable character. She had good manners, was rather extroverted and a sincere, warm-hearted person within. She generally got on with most but struggled with one significant relationship in her life, that with her mother. She loved her mother dearly who was by all accounts a most loving, sweet, gentlewoman.

Growing up Lucy found that she and her mother struggled to communicate together. Lucy recounted that they would argue fairly frequently and that this was often due to rather petty things. It seemed as though there was a constant unnecessary mismatch in their understanding of one another resulting in persistent conflicts. The conflicts may have been trivial but their frequency was damaging the enjoyment their relationship could and should have brought at the time.

Upon reflection, in her personal development journal, Lucy came to the realisation that her non-verbal behaviour was affecting how her mother was responding. This new understanding led to Lucy testing her theory by consciously behaving in a way that would invite positive behaviour and she soon realised that she was the one creating the animosity in their communication, not her mother. This understanding turned their relationship from unnecessarily tempestuous to calm and loving.

When you struggle to communicate with ease with a person you care for it can be extremely stressful. Those thoughts of why you can't have a conversation together without arguing, pop into mind. You wonder where it's all going wrong. Why you can't stop bickering. Why he takes everything you say in the wrong way. Why she doesn't realise you're just trying to help.

When you step back from the situation you can begin to wonder whether it is you that's starting the arguments or them. If you are experiencing this with a few individuals then it is likely that the fault lies with you as you are the common denominator in those relationships. If it is only happening with one person then the answer becomes less clear.

The bottom line is you want to resolve it. You may well be the innocent party far more than the creator of the conflict but the fact is that *you* can only change how *you* are functioning within the given relationship. Therefore, that is where you look to make a change or maybe just some tweaks.

In the true story of Lucy and her mother, Lucy discovered that people respond and react to the way another person communicates with them. She found that by approaching her conversations with her mother differently she drew different outcomes. Sometimes we can get so carried away with our feelings of self-righteousness and/or self-pity that we forget to look at the messages we are sending out to others.

Now let's think back to what we were discussing earlier on in Chapter 4, where we looked at how we interpret previous events which then create feelings that feed our proceeding behaviour. When you consider how a repetition of arguments with the same person can have a knock-on effect on how you relate to that person the next time you communicate, you may begin to see that perhaps you are not being as warm, affectionate or as reasonable as you thought.

Example -------------------------------------
Terry and his long-term romantic partner Kate have began bickering for apparently no reason whatsoever. They feel in a rut and both believe the other is in the wrong. The arguments are usually over trivial things such as cleaning the counter in the kitchen or taking the bins out or deciding on what to do together at the weekend or the way the other person spoke. The simplest conversation creates animosity.

One day Kate asks Terry to do something to which he replies, "I will."

"What is your problem? You always have attitude when I ask you to do anything?"

Kate is thinking of all the previous occasions where she has recently asked Terry to do something around the house and she feels her request has been met with annoyance.

Terry replies, "What? You just asked me to bring the cups down to the kitchen when I come down and I said I will! You're the one with the attitude!"

Is it possible that Kate is unfairly judging Terry's response to her latest question based on her interpretation of how he has responded to similar questions in the recent past?

Is it possible that Kate is displaying a bad attitude and Terry is not or vice versa?

Is it possible that Kate and Terry are both being stand-offish in their demeanour?

Yes, yes, and yes. All of the above could be true. Here's the thing - unless you are a party to the communication, or at least present, you cannot fairly judge who is being how. *Even if you are involved* you cannot always do so. The simple fact is that everyone perceives the world through their own subjective view. That view is invariably based on previous experiences, how those were interpreted, the feelings that developed as a result, how those feelings fed your resulting behaviour, the results that are subsequently received, the way that you interpret those results/experiences, and so on. The cycle goes on and on and on. The cycle that Kate and Terry are on includes recent argument after argument after argument. Each quarrel feeds the perceptions, and thus feelings, of the next. One incident in isolation will normally be treated as a one-off. However, if the negative cycle continues, it creates a gradually increasing problem that *seems* to get bigger and bigger, a bit like a snowball as you continue to roll it through fresh snow. It's just layer upon layer of negative interpretations that increase the size of the problem. Just as the sun melts away the layers of a snowball, a conscious effort to alter one's perception can melt away the layers of recent negatively perceived communications.

Kate is feeling bitter about the recent events that she has perceived as problematic, negative communications between her and Terry. She is carrying that memory into her future communications as is evident from her comment: "You always have attitude when I ask you to do anything?" When she is having a new conversation she is still holding her memories of the old ones at the forefront of her mind. This can then affect how she perceives the new communication she receives in response to her latest request of bringing the cups to the kitchen. When you are already expecting a negative response before you've even asked your question you can easily perceive a non-offensive response as being offensive. It becomes a self-fulfilling prophecy. You expect it to be so and as a result it becomes so. Or rather, you make it so in your perception. However, which came first, the negative response or the expectation of a negative response? Each situation is different and it's up to you to ask yourself if deep down you were expecting a certain response/behaviour in a given situation. Do you perceive negativity in your problematic relationship because you are expecting the problems to exist? Are there more problems in your mind than in the reality of the relationship?

The way you verbally communicate your feelings will also determine the outcome. In an article published in the journal *Monitor on Psychology* (2011) the author references research undertaken by husband and wife team, John and Julie Gottman. One interesting finding was that happily married couples tend to communicate in a way that takes ownership of feelings rather than levelling accusations at the partner. For example, instead of saying, "You always leave your dirty dishes in the bedroom. You obviously don't care about anyone but yourself," this can be better communicated with, "It upsets me to see your dirty dishes repeatedly left in the bedroom." By stating how you feel within yourself, rather than how you feel towards the other person, you will make the recipient more receptive to what you wish to communicate. By not attacking the other person you are being non-offensive and, therefore, your communication will be better heard. This will result in a more harmonious relationship as you will be communicating positively and respectfully and you will thus be able to elicit the behaviour you desire.

Another element to evaluate in this type of predicament is *your* behaviour and how you are conveying yourself to the other party. In the true story at the beginning of the chapter, Lucy recognised that by altering her way of communicating with her mother she successfully altered the way they related to one another, thus improving their relationship.

Can you think of occasions where you have believed yourself to have been completely decent in your manner with someone only to realise in hindsight that perhaps you had not quite been so? What was it that you noticed? Did you recall the frown on your face, the tone of your voice, your preoccupation with another matter or your hand gestures?

There are many ways in which we communicate with a person, the majority of it being non-verbal. That means you are communicating with not only the words you speak but with the tone in your voice, the volume you use when speaking, the expression on your face, the gestures you make, the posture you hold and the look in your eyes. So often I have heard people say, "I only said..." when they haven't acknowledged what they also said non-verbally. Considering more than fifty percent of what we say is non-verbal such an oversight could be holding you back from relating well with others.

Some will try to be clever by saying something in a pleasant way but demonstrating with their non-verbal communication that they are, with all intention, being insincere or even cruel. This can be even more offensive and harmful to a relationship because it is deceitful. It is not difficult to tell when someone is being insincere or cruel on the inside whilst displaying kindness on the outside because the non-verbal communication usually gives the game away.

If you want to build a successful relationship with somebody you need to ensure that your verbal and non-verbal communications are saying the same thing *and* that they are inviting the response you desire.

Going back to the example of Terry and Kate, when Kate asks Terry to perform a task and then accuses him of having a bad attitude, her focus is on his communication.

If Kate looks at how she is communicating she may discover that she made her verbal request with a fed-up tone of voice or an aggressive one or an irate one. She may have spoken in an argumentative manner. She may have held a very sour face when making her request. She may have had a frown on her forehead, angry eyes, a clenched jaw or pursed lips. She may have been waving her arms around, slapping the back of one hand into the palm of the other, or stood with arms apart facing both palms towards each other with fingers outstretched. It is also possible that she had her arms crossed tightly, perhaps doing so as she uttered her request, placed a hand on her forehead, placed her hands on her hips, or placed her hands on the back of her neck with the fingers interlocked.

The list of non-verbal cues Kate may have given is a long one. Those mentioned here can be a sign of dismay, anger, aggression or disrespect. If Kate has at the stage of asking a question communicated in any of these negative non-verbal ways then she is clearly making an assumption about the response she will receive. Sound familiar?

Remember, at this stage Kate is asking her question not reacting to an answer and, therefore, any negative non-verbal communication must be in response to her own thoughts not the response given, right? Right. She may be expecting a negative response and so communicates in a way that reacts to a negative response *before it has even occurred*. What type of response does she then get to her negative assumption? A negative one, of course! She receives that which she expects.

In this type of situation it matters not what Terry says verbally or non-verbally, Kate may have already decided how she will interpret or react to the response she is about to receive, albeit without intention.

This scenario can happen to the best of us because we sometimes get carried away with our thoughts of previous events without giving the other person the benefit of a clean slate. What this can then do is filter through our non-verbal communication making a simple conversation into a confrontation. When you are in a communication rut in a relationship of yours you need to give the person, be it yourself or someone else, the benefit of the doubt. You must not expect negativity of yourself based on previous experiences no more than you should of anyone else. That is to say, don't evaluate yourself before you have taken action and when you have base it on its own merits, and do the same with others. Don't tell yourself I am going to mess this up or he is going to mess this up, be positive in what you expect from yourself and others and you'll stand the best chance of building a positive relationship with yourself and them.

You need to take control of your thoughts and expect positive outcomes as they, often subconsciously, affect your body language. No matter what you say "politely" or "pleasantly" your body language will do some of the talking for you.

It is also important to remember that your posture and body language feed your mental state and, therefore, it can determine your emotions. By utilising this knowledge you can relax your mind which will in turn relax your body language enabling you to communicate better with others.

Right now just stand up straight, look directly ahead, keep your back and shoulders straight and smile a big smile.

Hold that for about ten seconds. How does that feel? Now sit down on a seat, let your arms hang either side, wipe any sign of a smile off your face, let your shoulders slump downwards and look downwards towards your thighs. Hold that pose for about ten seconds. How does that feel? If you have followed these instructions fully there is no doubt you will answer in the same way as every person who tries these two positions. The body language in the former position will have induced a good feeling and the body language in the latter position will have induced a bad feeling. That's the power of body language. It can make you feel good or bad and it can make the other person feel good or bad. It can be determined by the rate at which you breathe, how you stand and sit, the expression on your face, the look in your eyes and the way you move or hold your body.

Some people like to stand when they are working as they find they can think better when stood upright. If you breathe steadily you relax your mind. If you smile you feel happier. If you raise your head up ever so slightly you feel confident. Raise it any further and you will convey arrogance and you could actually *feel* arrogant if your head *was* cocked up that high.

By controlling your body language you can assist a change in your thoughts. For example, you can help yourself to relax when feeling tense in a confrontational situation with someone.

By controlling your body language you can also mask some of the anger that you may be feeling when you are struggling to diffuse it. This is not a way to dupe people but rather to protect them from some of the anger and frustration that you may otherwise unintentionally convey too aggressively. Furthermore, if you are aggressive when communicating with the other person, chances are you will end up in an argument where no one's a winner and all you are left with is unnecessary tension between you. By bearing this in mind when communicating with others you will know how to help yourself communicate effectively and how to elicit a positive response from them.

So it works both ways: body language can be evaluated by others (and yourself) to determine your thoughts and emotions, regardless of what you are saying verbally, and you can help control your thoughts and emotions by controlling your body language. A smile with wide eyes does not say happy as much as it does scary (and a bit weird) but a smile coupled with warm, smiling eyes does spell happy. Furthermore, once the other party has evaluated your verbal and non-verbal language they will respond accordingly. As Lucy discovered, by changing how you respond to others, they will respond differently to you. Sometimes this takes a concentrated, forced effort that can feel contrived. As time goes by, what you begin with conscious effort later becomes habit. By so doing you will form a natural new way of communicating together, namely a calmer manner. Consequently, once the wheels of the new way of communicating are in motion, you can steer away from your communication rut and into a happier, healthier relationship.

When you master this change and thus reap the reward of relating better to those important to you it fuels a sense of pride in oneself. You will feel in control and skilled at communication. This is extremely empowering. You will then find yourself more at ease when broaching a difficult (or not-so-difficult) conversation with somebody.

If you are very clear in your mind of what you want the outcome to be then you can ensure your verbal and non-verbal communication is conducive to you receiving it.

Action Point ---------------------------------
Write an honest account of how you feel you have been communicating with the person/people you want to improve your relationship(s) with. Be sure to include both your verbal and non-verbal communication.

Secondly, write down how you would likely respond if someone communicated in that way with you.

Do you feel you would get a better response if you communicated differently? If so, describe how you will modify your current way of communicating in order to elicit your desired response.

Now act upon your suggestions for modified communication methods.

Chapter 12

Is It Me Or Is Everything Red?

"The best argument is that which seems merely an explanation."

- Dale Carnegie

How many times have you had an argument with someone important in your life and afterwards said to yourself, "Well that didn't go the way I expected!" or "I wish I had remembered to make those two specific points" or "I wish I had handled that differently"?

We all get into arguments or "heated discussions" with the people we love from time to time. Arguments happen, they happen for all sorts of reasons and as long as they are not frequent they are a healthy part of your relationships. Arguments help us to understand what others want and expect from us and also help us to clear the air. Sometimes the argument can be about the silliest thing and yet its real purpose is to release tension that has stemmed from numerous minor irritations.

When arguments and disagreements begin to permeate your once happy relationship on a frequent basis they are a clear tell-tale sign that your relationship has veered off the course of harmony and onto a rugged track. The *way* in which you set about redirecting the course of your relationship can be the accelerator to success or decline.

More people than one might expect have the ability to become quite irate when an argument takes place. Their temper can feel out of control, they might be prone to waving their hands in the air, shouting, throwing things and slamming doors. When this type of person is arguing with someone who speaks quietly, keeps their arms fairly stationary and does not throw or slam anything, an onlooker will often feel compelled to side with the more composed person. The calmer looking person may well be in the wrong, and by a mile, but their demeanour and composure will work in their favour.

When you display aggression in the form of a loud voice or throwing, slamming or punching objects you will struggle to win your argument and yet you are in it to win it, are you not? Behaving in such a fashion suggests a lack of respect for the other person even if you do not mean for it to. Even if the only reason you are behaving in this way is because it is the manner in which you currently release your pent up tension, it is still disrespectful towards the other person. When you exhibit aggression in the aforementioned way you are inadvertently telling the other person that you intend to threaten or cause pain, harm or humiliation; not exactly the way to get your point across, is it?

What does a display of aggression instantly do? It leads to the other person becoming defensive. What happens when someone becomes defensive? They are wholly determined to prove you wrong rather than listen to your side of the story. Once someone has become defensive they are no longer interested in hearing *your* case, they will usually want to put *their* case forward (fight) or leave the situation altogether (flee).

When you are having an argument that appears to be going nowhere the thing you need to recognise as quickly as you can is what it is that you are saying or doing, verbally or non-verbally, that is preventing you from achieving your desired results. You have a goal when you start your argument. You may want your child to talk to you with more respect, you may want your mother to treat you like the adult that you are or perhaps you want your partner to spend more quality time with you. Whatever your goal is, be sure to remember it and then use that as your focal point for moving forward. With your eye on the goal remember to watch your verbal and non-verbal language and constantly assess whether or not it is conducive to you achieving your desired result. If you want to be firm with a child to discipline them for unacceptable behaviour then being flimsy and laid back will not assist you. Therefore, you would need to ensure that the look in your eyes and the tone of your voice told the child that you mean business. If on the other hand you wanted to tell your friend that you were fed up of being taken for granted you would want to demonstrate your air of self-assuredness without coming across as arrogant or needy. You would want your verbal and non-verbal communication to say, "I deserve better and I am confident of this fact and believe myself to be on a level standing to you, not above, not below." In either of these examples aggressive behaviour will not bring about the desired results. Some self-control goes a long way.

Some of you will be sat there thinking about how incredibly difficult it can be to stay calm whenever you have an argument, either in general or with a particular person. Perhaps you can feel overwhelmed by anger and feel as though your "head is about to explode". You may feel that to be calculated in how you deal with arguments feels unnatural, and maybe even contrived, but arguments are like a sales pitch.

Before a sales pitch takes place a good salesperson will have, at the very least, an idea of what he wants to say, he will know what the desired outcome of the sales pitch is, he will rehearse his script in advance to improve his chances of closing the deal and as he repeats this process he will become a better salesperson and produce more sales over time. Winning an argument is a similar process. If you have at the very least an idea of what you want to say, know what the desired outcome of your argument is, and rehearse what you are going to say and how you are going to deliver your argument in advance, you will more likely succeed in putting your point across and achieving your desired results. As you repeat this process you will become more successful at winning your arguments and, therefore, win them more frequently over time. That's what you want after all, isn't it? Nobody has an argument with the intention of losing it. Like a salesperson, over time you will learn the techniques to win and winning will become second nature rather than the contrived, mechanical methodology you will have applied in days gone by.

There are a number of elements to master in order to put your case forward respectfully, have your argument truly heard and acknowledged, and persuade the other party that your point of view is correct or at least as equally valid as theirs.

One of the main requirements is a calm composure. When you are calm the other person will be less defensive and they will be more likely to listen to and actually *hear* whatever it is that you are trying to convey. When you are calm during your argument you inadvertently tell the other party that you are confident of your standpoint. You are suggesting that you don't need to add effect to what you are saying because you know you have a sound argument and your words are themselves sufficient for conveying your message.

Staying calm when you are feeling wound up, and approaching an argument in a calm manner, is not always as easy as it sounds and so here are seven useful tips that can help:

- Breathing steady sends a message to your brain that you are feeling calm and can thus help you to reach a calm state.
- Smile to yourself even if you don't feel like smiling. Again your body will signal to your brain that you feel happier which will assist in calming you down.
- Exercise. This may take the form of walking, jogging/running, lifting weights or doing some housework. Some will find the exertion of energy through the pushing of weights can help to release tension. Others will find that cleaning the house can expel the negative energy by channelling the energy outwards through this act. What you need to do is find the energy release that suits you, whether that is some form of physical exercise or some form of housework.
- Creativity such as writing, drawing or playing an instrument can assist as an outlet of tension.
- Writing a letter or email addressed to the "perpetrator" about the way you *feel* can be a massive help although you must not actually send this letter/email to the other party. It is solely to

vent your frustrations, your anger and gain clarity regarding how you have perceived a situation, how you really feel about it, what you wish to convey to the other party and what your desired outcome is. Therefore, this technique of writing a letter or message has a two pronged effect; it helps to dispel the tension and calm the mind and it helps one to formulate a clear, intelligent argument in advance of any discussions taking place with the other party, similar to a sales pitch being created as per the comparison earlier.

- Talk to someone that is impartial, trustworthy and non-judgemental if you can. Similar to the writing of a letter or message this too can be cathartic as you share your thoughts and feelings with someone else.
- Allow time to lapse. This may not be a technique for instant calming and releasing of tension but over time one can feel calmer, clearer and better able to broach the subject of one's argument with the other person. The lapsing of time allows reflection. It allows you to look at your argument from all angles. It also allows you to look at the counter argument from differing angles, whether the counter argument has previously been proposed or whether the response to your argument is at this stage imagined based on your prior knowledge and expectations.

When you have mastered your feeling of serenity prior to broaching an argument or if you have at the very least calmed down somewhat, you should now consider the best time to have your discussion.

- Always ensure there is plenty of time to have your discussion. There is little point in having the discussion when there will not be sufficient time to resolve your issue. The cutting short of such a conversation will only further aggravate your feelings and possibly the feelings of the other party and the situation may become worse.
- Ensure the other party is not already pre-occupied with other concerns. For example, if the other person is worried about a project at work or particularly worried about a loved one's ill health then an ill-timed argument is likely to be perceived as hurtful, inconsiderate and selfish. You will struggle to get your point across and you will paint yourself in a bad light. Besides, if you love the person, putting your needs aside, you would surely want to limit the amount of stress they were under rather than add to it.
- Ensure you have their full attention. If you do not you will more likely get frustrated and the argument could turn much nastier than necessary because of the added insult you might endure of feeling you are being ignored or disregarded. In addition, if the other person only catches part of what you are saying they will not necessarily understand the point you wish to make. The other party's undivided attention can be gained by switching off the TV or music, asking them to close their laptop or put their phone down and requesting that they face you and look into your eyes.
- Have the argument in privacy. If you care for and love the person you are confronting then you do

not want to humiliate them. Even if in your moment of anger you feel that you do it is unlikely that you will still feel this way when you have calmed down so be mindful of behaving respectably.

When you have the argument itself there are a few simple points to bear in mind regarding your communication:

- If you do not know the techniques used by orators to influence a crowd then keep your body language simple. Keep your arms, legs, feet, hands and head as relaxed as possible and to play it safe keep their movements gentle and occasional rather than aggressive and frequent. Many great orators do not distract from what they are saying with too much body movement, and they will ensure it backs up what they are saying verbally. By keeping your body language steady you neither risk aggravating the situation (with potentially negative or aggressive non-verbal communication) nor do you overwhelm the other person thus forcing them to retreat mentally and physically from the discussion. Your eyes are one of the major focal points during a conversation. Be sure to hold eye contact with the other person but be gentle with your eyes if you want to be heard. The saying "the eyes are the window to the soul" should be remembered. If you have a look that says "I'm ready to rip your head off", so to speak, you will only be defeating your own purpose. Aggressive eyes will not help the other person to want to listen to what you have to say, it will mentally turn them off. If you are finding it incredibly difficult during an argument to show anything but contempt for the other party (as you cannot shed your aggressive thoughts) then it can be helpful to avert your gaze until you feel calmer and then regain your eye contact with them. Sometimes this can be done by offloading a few more sentences to release some of the tension building up within. As you manage to voice your opinion more you will feel calmer as you progress closer to your objective.

- The volume of your voice should neither be too loud nor too quiet. If you speak too loud you convey aggression, if you speak too quiet you convey a lack of assuredness in what you are saying. Either way you will harm your desired outcome.
- Keep the tone as steady and respectful as possible. The tone of the voice can convey so very many things. In that moment it can convey how meek you are, how aggressive you are being, whether you are being arrogant, condescending, delirious, dismissive, disrespectful or despondent to name a few.
- Use polite, respectful language. Absolutely try to refrain from using any swear words whatsoever. Even if you are swearing mid-sentence rather than swearing at the other person, it will make the other person defensive, thus undermining your efforts, and you will look unpleasant and immature.

When embarking on a heated discussion, debate or argument (whatever you wish to call it) it can be easy to make a bad situation worse if you do not control your temper, the environment, your behaviour, the timing and the other party's attention.

Whilst arguments can be uncomfortable they do help you to reach an understanding between yourself and the other person. Sometimes an argument will actually help you tighten the bond you have with someone and that is priceless. However, you may be finding that arguments are not having the desired effect and/or you may be struggling to master the above techniques because you are so enraged by whatever it is that is causing the disagreements. In such a case a drastic change in approach can result in the other party really paying attention to what you are feeling and trying to convey.

If someone is used to you arguing, a sudden silent, non-argumentative and subdued stance can really make the other party sit up and pay attention. As it is not what they are used to they will notice the change quite quickly. There is nothing offensive about a person being quiet and distant either and it can attract the other person towards you. Reducing your communication right down to a minimum speaks volumes. Becoming withdrawn and subdued lets the person know you are hurting but not trying to hurt them. This is not something that should be mistakenly used in conjunction with self-pity nor am I suggesting that you put on a false act. Sincerity is one of the most important principles one should live one's life by and it is absolutely vital for healthy, successful relationships. What I am saying is that the internalisation of your sadness and anger, as opposed to the vocalising of it, can assist in getting your argument heard eventually. The act of taking this quiet, solemn approach can also draw *you* towards feeling calmer; it can bring clarity and thus help you to handle the situation more constructively. It does not prevent you from implementing the techniques mentioned above to release the tension building up within, they are still useful. It simply means you channel your emotions in a different direction, inwards instead of outwards. Once you have gained clarity, composure and the other's undivided attention you can communicate your feelings and go on to achieve your objective of being truly heard.

If you are going to argue, argue well, be respectful, keep your cool, think about what you are doing and remember what you set out to achieve.

Action Point ----------------------------------
In written format describe which aspects of the way you argue/debate work against your objective of conveying your point of view, i.e. what you do that you *shouldn't do* for your own sake of being heard.

Next write details of what you *will do* from now on to improve the effectiveness of how you argue/debate so that both parties gain from it and both are treated with respect so that, consequently, your relationship grows stronger.

Finally, implement the intended changes that you have explored here.

Chapter 13
Changing Without Aggravating

"Behaviour is the mirror in which everyone shows their image."

- Johann Wolfgang von Goethe

It can be incredibly easy to bicker over the most trivial issues when you live with someone else. Even though parents tend to exercise more patience with their children, when it comes to two people cohabiting together (two adults or adult and child) tiny matters can become a recipe for unnecessary disputes. However, it has to be remembered that there are actions and then there are responses to those actions. Which one do you think has the compounding effect on the decline of a relationship? It's the latter, of course. It's not what happens that affects us in life; it's how we respond to what happens that determines the outcome.

Whether we are building a relationship with someone new in our lives or maintaining an existing relationship, we need to manage the expectations we have of one another. To elaborate, following on is a case study of an adult-adult relationship.

Case Study ----------------------------------
A male named "Larry" embarked upon the journey of settling into a small local firm as a new employee. From the very first interview with the company, before Larry was

hired, he attempted to charm his way into the vacancy with his words and a somewhat over-confident manner. For some of those present at the interview stage the disparity between the spoken words and the actions that followed seemed immediately clear.

What became frustrating for some of the workforce was Larry's lack of effort to share the workload when large projects were taking place that required all staff to partake in additional duties. Initially the staff, and management alike, refused to make too much of it, considered the fact that he was still new to the company and was getting used to the company work ethic. They wanted Larry to feel settled and welcomed into their rather close knit workforce and did not want to create unnecessary upheaval. They gave him the benefit of assuming that once he had settled in he would naturally partake in shared duties around the workplace when major projects took place.

As time progressed what became especially noticeable was the fact that Larry would pull his weight in front of the managing director but often barely bother to lift a finger in front of the rest of the management and other staff members. This stark contrast spoke volumes to the workforce as it suggested Larry knew that he *should* be helping out more but only felt it necessary to do so in front of the managing director. Inadvertently, his behaviour demonstrated a lack of respect and consideration for the other staff members, management and subordinates. It showed Larry to be insincere and mildly manipulative. Clearly, his behaviour also insulted the intelligence of the others as they could clearly see this game of "keeping up appearances" that was being played out in front of solely the managing director.

Four months passed by and still nothing had changed. Larry had not taken the initiative to participate equally in the sharing of the workload as the workforce had hoped. One day, after a month of barely lifting a finger whilst the managing director was away on business, the very day the boss returned to work at the office, Larry decided to take on one of the larger duties, a task he had never once done out of choice. Upon noting this contrived persona being displayed, one of the employees, "Rob", decided to make a comment, in jest, but one that simply made a point of letting Larry know that his intentional lack of effort had not gone unnoticed. The comment was most likely a difficult pill to swallow and Larry is likely to have felt discontented, however, from that moment on he began to pull his weight noticeably more.

The comment had been made, Larry had taken note, and the relationship between him and Rob remained as it had been. If anything, both parties made slightly more effort with one another following the conversation.

The workforce agreed that something needed to be verbalised and were glad that something had been said. They were neither fools nor foes. They simply understood that there was a misbalance that required adjustment before bad behaviour became uncontrollable (and deemed acceptable by Larry) and before bitterness towards Larry developed and led to tensions. The workforce was, as mentioned, extremely tight knit. They were unwilling to allow any one person to upset the delicate balance of mutually respectful relationships they had fostered.

When it comes to human relationships we have to let people know what we expect of them if they are to be involved in our lives. You deserve to be treated with respect and consideration. Nobody wants to surround themselves with people who cannot honour these principles. Therefore, **we need to ensure that those in our lives deserve a place there.** For those who despite our efforts remain an unwelcome part of our lives, whether we like it or not, we simply need to practise keeping them at a distance, for example, an unpleasant sibling or parent. We'll revisit this distancing of harmful relationships in a latter chapter, for now we shall concentrate on managing relationships to create an experience we deserve.

The term managing relationships is something one should always consider when a relationship is not panning out the way intended or desired. The word "managing" instantly reminds you that you are in control, you have the ability to influence, you are the architect of the relationships you have. **Relationships are the result of each party's expectations.** You let the other person know what you expect and what you are willing to accept. Let me repeat that. **You let the other person know what you expect and what you are willing to accept.** The messages you send out signal to the other person what they can and cannot get away with in their relationship with you. Whether it's a parent and child, two partners, two siblings, two friends, two work colleagues, a boss and an employee or even a shop assistant and a customer, **you always convey through your verbal and non-verbal communication and your actions what you expect and are willing to accept.**

If someone in your life persistently treats you with indifference, you are allowing them to do so and you are thus telling them you accept it. If someone in your life repeatedly treats you with disrespect, by repeatedly condoning it you are teaching them that it is acceptable for them to do so. If someone hits you and you allow this aggressive behaviour to continue you are signalling to them that this abuse is acceptable. Do you see the pattern here? It works both ways. If someone treats you with respect, you have signalled to them that this is what you expect and accept from them. So before you look at how you can amend somebody's behaviour towards you have a look at the role *you have played* in allowing a culture of indifference, disrespect, abuse, or whatever it is, to have developed.

When you see those you have relationships with behaving in a way with you that you do not desire, you need to use evaluation followed by introspection and then modification.

Evaluation is first and foremost a way for you to see patterns of behaviour that may have formed over months or years. Look at reasons for the pattern of behaviour:

- Why are they behaving in this way?
- What does their behaviour tell you about them as a person?
- What does it say about their relationship with you?

To demonstrate a quick evaluation let us review the case of Larry. It would appear that he was behaving in this manner because it allowed him to maintain his lazy disposition. His behaviour told those concerned that he wanted to portray himself in a positive light but lacked the drive to follow through with action. His behaviour also suggested, as previously mentioned, an element of insincerity and an attempt to push boundaries. What Larry's behaviour suggested about his relationship with his work colleagues was that he lacked the correct amount of respect *and* regard for them and considered them gullible and easy prey.

Once you have evaluated the other's behaviour, introspection becomes vital for you to understand how you feel about what you are experiencing and the role you have played in this behaviour that you are, in this instance, mentally condemning. "Why are they behaving in this way?" now becomes:

- Why do they think they can behave in this way?
- How do you feel about them behaving in this way?

This contemplative stage of the process can take time to work through. Whilst you may be able to answer the major points of this quite rapidly it can sometimes take longer to fully comprehend your own feelings about the behaviour and how you may have contributed. Take all the time that you need as you do not want to cause undue damage to the relationship or to other closely linked relationships as a result of moving too hastily into the final stage of modification. In the example of Larry, his colleague who confronted him took four months to evaluate what Larry's behaviour was signalling, what the workforce was doing to perpetuate it and how they felt about it. This is not to suggest that four months is necessary but if it requires four months then so be it. If you do not have four months to spend then you at least understand that careful critical evaluation and introspection is required before any haste is taken.

When you feel in your gut that the other person is definitely behaving in manner "x" and that you have responded with behaviour "y" and feel emotion "z" about it, you are then ready to enter the modification stage. The modification stage is where you decide what you will do to modify either the other person's behaviour or the situation. Remember though, to change the other person's behaviour you will also need to change what you are doing, whether it is something you are saying or not saying or whether it is something you are doing or not doing. The introspection stage will assist you in determining what needs to change in order for the outcome to change. For example:

- Do you need to speak up or do you speak up too much and need to keep quiet?
- Do you always give in and now need to stand firm with your principles or are you so hard faced that a softer tactic will elicit the desired effect?
- Are you inconsistent with your actions and need to create consistency?

When you have determined how you have contributed to the problem as you see it you can then modify your behaviour, thus modifying the other person's behaviour and creating the results you desire.

In the case of Larry, at this point there was a lack of effort during large work projects; tomorrow there could have been a lack of effort for vitally important business meetings or a lack of effort within Larry's own workload. By deciding to make one comment, this one single change in the behaviour of the aggrieved, resulted in a change in Larry's behaviour in the direction of the desired outcome. One slight amendment not only changed the desired outcome concerning the presenting issue it also laid some of the foundation for the relationship's future. Therefore, further derailment of the relationship between Larry and the rest of the workforce was prevented whilst simultaneously allowing the workforce to reassert their power in the relationship, reinstating the equilibrium.

Dealing with undesirable behaviour is a natural part of relating to one another. As you can see from the case of Larry, great care had to be taken to delicately weave the relationship towards the direction of mutual respect, trust, commitment, communication and friendship. This is the case with all relationships that are important to you. Modification is the part of the process that can make or break relationships. One can evaluate and look introspectively within one's own mind but to modify the behaviour of someone towards a more desirable experience can be fraught with dangers due to its involvement of the other person.

When looking at ways to modify the other person's behaviour one must, as previously discussed, look at how one is perpetuating the situation, if at all. If it transpires that you are not saying anything when you experience a certain undesirable behaviour that you wish to alter, what are you inadvertently telling that person? Usually this lets the perpetrator know that their behaviour is acceptable.

There is a difference between not wanting to give someone attention for bad behaviour (if attention is what they are seeking) and not actually letting them know that their behaviour is unacceptable. There are ways you can do both. For example, by failing to watch the behaviour you can opt to avert your attention, or actually leave the room, each time they act in the undesirable way. By so doing you are letting them know that you do not approve whilst at the same time you are not giving them the attention they desire either. This is a non-verbal way of letting them know, with your actions, that you do not approve of their behaviour.

You can of course be more forthright and simply tell a person that you do not approve if you are finding that by not saying anything somebody's behaviour is getting worse and/or out of control. This entails careful planning if you want to elicit the necessary adjustment in behaviour *and* avoid any negative repercussions. In the case of Larry, his colleague told him in jest, after four months, that his lack of effort had not gone unnoticed. Had his colleague been more direct or had the comment been made at all aggressively or disrespectfully, Larry could have retaliated instead of taking the comments on board and somewhat amending his behaviour accordingly. If the same point had been made in the wrong way then Larry's relationship with his colleagues could have been affected as could the relationship of Rob and his colleagues. Plus, Larry could have ignored the statement and not changed his behaviour, regardless of whether he agreed or not, simply out of hurt, anger or belligerence.

When you want to say something to alert someone of your disapproval of their behaviour, again you need to take into account the following:

- the words you are using,
- the body language you are using,
- the tone of your voice,
- what the main issue is,
- what the desired outcome is,
- keeping the message succinct.

By using gentle words the recipient will find it easier to truly listen to what you have to say and you do not need to portray yourself as an ogre. By using words that suggest you disapprove of the behaviour rather than the person you are also dealing an easier blow. Humour can also be a great tool for communicating what needs to be said. It makes the whole conversation much easier and feel lighter. People tend to be more receptive to humour than a serious conversation as the humour helps the recipient of the comments to relax which assists them in hearing what you are saying without feeling the need to be as defensive about it.

You may even decide to write a funny handwritten note or a cute note so that it is less confrontational and appeals to them with its humour or sweetness. For example, I have at times written notes to my husband to remind him of something that he needs to do when he repeatedly fails to do it despite my numerous requests. Rather than feel as though I am constantly badgering him about the same thing and so that he does not feel as though he is being nagged by me about the same thing repeatedly, I will sometimes replace my spoken words with a note. Writing a note is not the best way to communicate with all people or during all circumstances but it certainly can be a good way to vary one's communication every now and again with certain people.

As a general rule, there needs to be closeness (and plenty of face-to-face communication) between you and the prospective recipient of your note for it to work effectively. In addition, the note needs to be written with a humorous, loving or endearing approach.

For example, I occasionally use notes with my husband, not all the time. Drawing is not my forte and so by scribbling little images for humour it not only makes my husband laugh but my poor artwork also endears him. Sometimes I will write the note as though the object I am referring to is writing the note. This makes the note cute rather than nasty and the injected humour makes the whole message easy to swallow. So if I want a pile of dishes washing I might draw a really bad picture of dirty dishes and then write something witty in the first person as though I am the dishes talking. Of course to use this method frequently would be overkill but to do it now and again can be extremely effective.

Your body language, as discussed in an earlier chapter, indicates your intentions, thoughts and feelings. Ensure that they are conducive to achieving your desired outcome of changing the other's behaviour without inviting negative repercussions. If necessary be assertive but do not be aggressive so that they do modify their behaviour.

When you have something to say and you want to achieve a certain result by saying it remember this key point when you are about to confront somebody about their undesirable behaviour: keep it as succinct as possible. No matter how pleasantly you convey your point it is still highlighting something the other person displeases you with, therefore, making your point must not be a dragged out affair. There is no podium; you are not giving a speech. Deliver a swift message, ensure they have heard what you have said and then change the subject to something completely unrelated and pleasant and light hearted if possible. This way you have successfully delivered your message and they feel uncomfortable for as little time as possible. This will make them more receptive to what you have said rather than defensive. The longer you take making a point, the more defensive they will become and the less effective your message will be. It is also important to remember that you do not want to embarrass them unduly so do ensure there is no audience present if possible. In fact, depending on the situation a third person can work for or against you and that is something you need to assess for yourself depending on the given situation. For example, if the person you are confronting is manipulative then a third person can be useful but *only* if you can trust them to remain impartial.

Saying something to someone can often be the best and sometimes the only way to communicate your expectation of a change in the other person's behaviour. However, if you are finding that everything you say is being ignored or creating animosity then you have to evaluate first of all if you are behaving in *all* of the ways suggested here. Perhaps your non-verbal communication is creating arguments when you are trying to talk to someone about a change you expect. Perhaps every inch of your communication is perfectly orchestrated for eliciting your desired outcome but maybe you are communicating it too often. If you can say, hand on heart, that you are communicating well and with the right frequency *or* if you suspect that your communication is great but you may be voicing your opinions and concerns too frequently then it may be time for a change in approach.

When you find your words failing to make the impact that you had hoped for upon a person's behaviour, silence can be highly effective. If someone feels that they are used to hearing you "nag" or "scold" them too often then they may begin to switch off when you start "nagging" or "scolding". Similarly, if they are feeling fed up or hurt by your comments they may consequently switch off when you begin talking as a form of defence - *if I don't listen I won't be hurt by it* type of mentality. This can result in bad behaviour continuing regardless of what you say and frustration, tension and resentment building up on both sides. For this reason, silence can be a very welcome change for both parties. The change can spark a dissipation of the negative energies (frustration, tension and resentment) and diminishing defensiveness. As the other person begins to feel more relaxed they become more receptive to what you are trying to ask them to do or change.

Now whilst I am talking about using silence this is a silence that is coupled with non-verbal cues as to what you want to convey, the thing that you usually do verbalise but that you are now saying non-verbally only.

Example ------------------------------------
Jason and Joe live together as adult father and son, respectively. Joe constantly leaves soiled clothes on the bathroom floor rather than placing them in the laundry basket. He does not listen to his father's repeated requests to change this behaviour.

To amend this behaviour Jason takes a new approach. He makes eye contact with Joe, immediately followed by a glance at the clothes on the floor and then glances back at Joe with a dismayed and saddened look in his eyes and on his face. He may not have spoken but his look tells Joe that he feels hurt and disappointed. As Joe loves Jason and does not want to be responsible for disappointing him and causing him pain, he quietly picks up the soiled clothes and places them in the laundry basket. When Jason later discovers this good behaviour he regains his jovial, loving demeanour with his son as a way of letting him know that the disagreement is now in the past and that he has made him happy. Joe knows he has done the right thing; he feels good about making Jason proud and happy and feels good for eliminating the negativity he was creating in their relationship.

When Joe intermittently repeats the behaviour of leaving soiled clothes on the bathroom floor his father sometimes verbalises his request and sometimes gives "the look". When he communicates with Joe regarding this matter he tends to feel more relaxed as he has now experienced his son obeying this rule on previous occasions. Therefore, Jason is more inclined to use relaxed, friendly, non-argumentative verbal and non-verbal communication when having to remind his son of his request. This then has a knock-on effect on how Joe responds to him and his requests. Each time victory is experienced by the father he responds kindly to his son. Each time his son receives this rewarding positive response from his father he feels good about having obeyed him. This knock-on effect bounces back and forth, all the while bettering the quality of their relationship and eliminating the bad behaviour.

Sometimes it just takes a look or an air of dissatisfaction to convey calmly and effectively what dozens of words cannot. It is also worth remembering that when you withdraw from someone it can draw them in towards you. If they care for you and notice you are withdrawing from them they will still want to maintain a relationship with you and so if you do not reach out for them, they will reach for you. This may not happen immediately but if you leave the relationship in a distant state that they are not used to they will use some mode of reaching out to reignite contact with you. The important thing for you to remember is having the strength and patience in waiting it out, so to speak.

Going back to the previous example of Jason and Joe, instead of solely using non-verbal communication the father may have communicated, verbally or non-verbally, *and* offered an incentive or reward. Jason could have conveyed his point non-verbally in the bathroom and then upon seeing that his son had corrected his behaviour he could have given him a more tangible reward than simply demonstrating his approval and satisfaction. If he felt the need to better reinforce Joe's good behaviour he might have said, "Come on son, because you have demonstrated maturity and respect for me I'm taking you out for lunch." This is a more blatant way of telling somebody that their changed behaviour is appreciated and the reward reinforces this message. This has the effect of making them want to repeat their good behaviour and eliminate the bad. A repetition of positive reinforcement over time will better the relationship experience. Of course you shouldn't have to reward people with meals or something else but sometimes it can be necessary if you are struggling to get what you want.

If you offer the reward as a surprise treat for someone improving their behaviour it lets you know that they did it for you and/or to do what's right, not for the reward. It can also have a bigger impact on the other party as they did not expect your reward. If you do offer the reward whilst requesting the change in behaviour it may result in the person changing their behaviour for the sake of a reward rather than out of respect for you or to do the right thing. However, if you do choose this method, as you follow through with the reward promised as well as the reward of responding to them positively and praising them for what they have done, this too will have a positive effect on your relationship in the manner described in the first example of Jason and Joe. Therefore, you must remember that a tangible reward may be useful when dealing with an especially difficult situation but the important factor comes back to how you make them feel with the way you relate to them as one human to another. Show them you love them, are proud of them, approve of their good behaviour and are happy about how they have obeyed your request, even if just with some words and a smile. This will positively feed their cycle of thoughts about their relationship with you.

One final point to make here about how you communicate verbally or non-verbally, with or without rewards, is that whatever messages you do communicate must remain consistent and whatever you do promise must be honoured.

Learn to respond to undesirable behaviour in a way that is conducive to positive change. You must first silently gather your facts so that you have conviction in your thinking. With that knowledge you can decide if the behaviour is unacceptable to you or just your misunderstanding. When you know for sure that something needs to change in order for your relationship to work better, ensure you respectfully and shrewdly induce a change in their behaviour.

Action Point ---------------------------------
Write an evaluation of the things that you want to see change in the way the other person behaves in their relationship with you.

Is it necessary for them to change these things in order for you to both have a mutually respectful, loving, happy relationship with one another?

If so, describe three ways you could approach each issue in a way that will successfully bring about the changes you desire so that you can improve your relationship.

Now take action on the approaches you have proposed.

Repeat the above process until you have successfully eliminated all undesirable behaviour from the relationship(s) you are intent on improving.

Chapter 14

The Role You Are Playing

"Human behaviour flows from three main sources: desire, emotion and knowledge."

- Plato

In the previous chapter we touched upon behaviour reinforcement. It can be said that people tend to look at what others are doing wrong before they acknowledge the part they have played and are playing in reinforcing their behaviour. As previously mentioned, people behave as you allow them to behave.

Within your life, your world, you create the rules that you live by. Sure, the government sets out its rules that govern the country and local area you live in but you choose whether or not to obey them. Similarly, employers define their rules and the employees work within those confines to achieve what they want to achieve.

Based on the rules we learn from our parents or other guardians we establish our own version of those rules, particularly as we grow older. When someone that you have an important relationship with begins to behave in a way that is unappealing, remember that you are responsible for enforcing your rules by either opposing or reinforcing that behaviour. It is also important to note that a lack of self-defence can be interpreted by the perpetrator as a green light for a situation to continue, i.e. as behaviour reinforcement.

Case Study -
Being the youngest of five children I have most definitely enjoyed some perks along the way. On the flip side being the youngest can bring a few difficulties, most of which I only recognised, and experienced, as I became an adult. One such difficulty was asserting the fact that I am no longer a child.

Despite being married, in my early thirties and mature for my age (since before becoming a teenager) some of my siblings failed to recognise the fact that I was now a young lady. After a number of incidents occurred spanning over seven months I began to look back at things that had been happening and things that had been said over the preceding few years (my late 20s to my early 30s). It became apparent to me that despite having demonstrated my maturity and level-headedness, some of the siblings were at times still dismissive of me, my opinions and my knowledge. As I reviewed the incidences of the seven month period it dawned on me that not once had my opinions been acknowledged despite having asserted myself. In fact I had found myself having to enlist the help of my parents or other siblings to help fight my battles for me, so to speak. They had to speak in my defence in order to relay my arguments so that they would actually be heard. How pathetic that felt!

Through the pain and frustration I found myself retreating from the dismissive siblings and the distance allowed me to process what had been happening and what was going wrong. It dawned on me that perhaps I needed to let them know that enough was enough, that I was now an adult and I expected the respect I deserved. I *had* been forthright with my opinions regarding the topics we had debated over the previous months, and years. What I *hadn't* done was something I didn't feel I should have to do, remind them that I was now a real adult. If I was going to have to spend my life getting other family members to reiterate my case for me I was never going to have the mutually respectful, loving relationships that I wanted with *all* of my siblings. Not only did it feel ridiculous to have others arguing on my behalf, they would not always be around to do so and nor did I want to put them in that position. The time had come to assert my adulthood to them for once and for all.

Some time away from the siblings in question allowed me to gather my thoughts. I decided I had been too soft whenever they had dismissed the now adult me. Not one for holding grudges I had previously debated my side of the discussions that had taken place and then quickly acted as though nothing had happened. Whilst this is a personality trait that I do not wish to alter I did need to send out the message that whilst I may be incredibly forgiving I am not to be ignored, dismissed or treated with disrespect, albeit unintentionally. In other words, *I had reinforced* this notion they had that I was not a fully fledged adult because I had not communicated the opposite clearly enough in my way of relating to them. Of course, had I not been the youngest of five children this probably wouldn't have been as necessary but when you are that far down the line and there is 13 years difference between you and the eldest, the family dynamic can be a much more complex and rigid one. The time away from the siblings also gave them time to digest my messages that conveyed that I too was an adult, and a self-assured one, who deserved to be treated as one. The distance was my way of also saying that if they did not want to treat me with deserved respect they would not have a relationship with me. That I would not simply act as though nothing had happened until they acknowledged that something needed to shift in their perception of me before we could resume our otherwise loving relationship. This was my way of *opposing* their undesirable behaviour. After less than one week of silence, no further messages and no contact, when I got in touch the response was one of acknowledgement for the hurt caused and their ensuing behaviour demonstrated their realisation that I was not to be dismissed as a child nor disrespected.

I knew that I would have to consistently convey this message for it to be fully accepted within their psyche but by reinforcing a message again and again it eventually brings a new way of behaving and relating. I had unknowingly spent a few years reinforcing the idea that it was okay to dismiss me as young and naive, even though I clearly wasn't. I would, therefore, have to undo the behaviour I had reinforced by opposing it and reinforcing the behaviours I desired.

The above is just one example of how we can reinforce how people behave with us and then suffer the consequences. If we don't recognise the part that we play we can forever try to change the other party's opinion or behaviour, however, if we don't stop reinforcing the undesirable and begin reinforcing the desirable, we have an uphill struggle on our hands.

In my case I hadn't particularly felt it necessary to be accepted as an adult and had, in fact, dismissed many incidences with a mental rolling of the eyes. I knew what they were thinking; I just didn't care because it didn't affect me, at that time. I had noticed the pattern and even recognised the reason for it, i.e. that being the youngest they still saw me as young even though I wasn't. I had found it interesting, even amusing, from a psychological perspective and simply enjoyed observing it. Only when it became evident that their mentality was hindering my life did I feel the need to actually create a mental shift in their minds by reacting to it differently from how I had been so far.

In other words, it may not have been an issue in the past and that may be why you have allowed a certain person to behave in a certain way. Once you recognise someone's behaviour is affecting you and your relationship, you will then need to look at the role you have and/or are playing in keeping that unwelcome behaviour alive.

If you do not set the expectations from the outset you are inviting unnecessary drama into your lives. It is worth remembering the saying that "old habits die hard". It is far better and easier to nip bad behaviour in the bud than to let it escalate or at least incubate for many years and then try to change it. This is important to remember whether you have invited someone new into your life, whether someone else has invited someone new into your life (their partner, for example), whether an existing relationship is evolving or if you have a change in lifestyle. It is easier to forget this when: someone else invites a third person into your life or an existing relationship evolves. However, if you are at that stage now whereby the bad behaviour has developed then you can apply the lessons within this book to help you reverse the programming.

Be aware that you can be reinforcing behaviour, in children *and* adults alike, with your response to it. You have to let people know what's acceptable in a relationship with you.

Action Point -
In written format identify the ways in which you have reinforced unwelcome behaviour in the relationship(s) you want to improve.

Now identify how you could alter your responses to invite a change in their behaviour that would result in a more desirable outcome.

Now act upon the proposed changes in the responses you give.

Chapter 15

Silently Loud

"Well-timed silence hath more eloquence than speech."

- Martin Farquhar Tupper

In the previous two chapters we have looked at the ways you can change someone's undesirable behaviour, in order to better your relationship, without worsening the situation. We also explored the fact that you need to look inwards at any contributions you have made that have reinforced the behaviour in question. It is now pertinent to expand on our previous discussion about the power of silence and the use of non-verbal communication.

If you recall the example of co-habiting father and son, Jason and Joe, you'll remember that we briefly touched upon the topic of silence and its ability to convey a point more effectively. Yes silence can bring calmness to a situation by reducing the tension that verbalising an issue can induce. Yes it has the ability to let people think more clearly and evaluate matters easier. Silence is also an incredibly powerful tool for allowing people to gage what they've done wrong or to let them know where they stand when it comes to their relationship with you. Silence can be a way for you to convey your contempt. Silence can let people know that you are paying attention. Silence can also be a way to let people know that you are not interested or not paying attention. Silence is indeed a powerful tool.

Charles DeGaulle once said, "Silence is the ultimate weapon of power." It certainly does carry immense power when used appropriately within a certain situation or with certain people. It is a tool that is probably not used enough by some assertive people and a tool used too often by some quiet people. Whether you are assertive or submissive you can benefit your relationships by using silence when it is used selectively, in the right proportion and in the right manner to achieve your desired outcome.

On a day to day basis we see many obvious examples of the power of silence. Many times we hear a salesman talk his way into and then out of a sale because he couldn't be silent. Sometimes a famous person will say too much, consequently get himself into "hot water" and all the while we can be left thinking why he didn't just stay silent. A child talks back when the respectful thing would have been to stay silent. An argument escalated because we couldn't stay silent. In our desire to be too honest without anticipating the backlash we spoke up and later wished we had remained silent. By verbally retaliating to someone being aggressive we lost our own credibility when the most effective thing would have been - to have stayed silent. There are most definitely circumstances in which silence can hold immense power and mastering such power can help you in your relationships.

To convey a point more effectively silence can be deafening, particularly when used by an assertive person. The fact that such a person has not verbalised what they are thinking and/or feeling can suggest that they are furious, dismayed, shocked, upset, jealous, unsure, unhappy, bored, or fearful, to name a few emotions. So how does one ensure that the correct message is being signalled to the recipient?

As we are looking at the management of relationships, silence in this context is not used in an isolated manner. As such you will be in communication with the recipient of your silence in one form or another over an extended period of time. Consequently, they will be aware of and understand your usual communication patterns.

When you couple a silence with telling non-verbal communication the message you wish to convey can become quite apparent. Crossed arms, a serious look in the eyes and a raised eye brow screams discontent, but you don't have to be so obvious with your non-verbal communication to let someone know what your silence means. It can be much more exhilarating to use silence with minimal non-verbal communication and still know that your message has been heard loud and clear.

Let us assume that you wish to tell someone that you are not impressed with their constant bragging and that you do not believe the lies that they tell you in order to portray themselves in a certain false way. Without having to utter any words you can silently ignore what they say and change the topic. By doing so you are not acknowledging what they have said. This can indicate to the other person that the bragging or the lies are insignificant. That you do not intend to dignify the nonsense that they come out with because you either do not approve of what they are saying or do not believe what they are telling you. It is difficult for someone to keep doing something that you repeatedly show your disapproval of. It becomes meaningless for someone to continue saying something to you that you do not appear to believe. You can stop a person from behaving in undesirable ways when they repeatedly see that you do not condone or approve of such behaviour, whatever the reason for your feelings. When they receive the same message repeatedly they will begin to retreat from such behaviour. The repetition and consistency in your response is what creates the change in their behaviour. This is because they will, over time, notice a pattern in your response and as you refuse to give their undesirable behaviour the response they are seeking their (bad) habit becomes useless.

What is so effective about this type of experience is that it is a relatively peaceful, confident, non-aggressive way of communicating what you want to say to, or even scream at, someone. So remember, if you consistently do not respond to something undesirable someone is saying or doing when by so doing they are seeking out a response from you, silence followed by a simple, polite change of subject can send your reply back loud and clear.

If someone is behaving aggressively, silence followed by a change of subject may aggravate the situation and so it can be better to simply stay silent. Whilst this too can aggravate the other person it does still carry a few benefits. It gives them little reason to retaliate as there is little to retaliate to. It also makes their aggressive display more palpable to themselves which can act as a shaming factor that shames them into retreating from such behaviour.

A silent response to what's been said (or done) followed by somewhat quieter than normal speech is a great way to say, "I'm disappointed" or "You've upset me".

Do you notice how the slightest change can indicate a different emotion? You can change the length of the silence or the type of non-verbal communication in order to convey a different message without saying anything untoward. For example, the longer the silence you use the more intense your message of disapproval can be.

When you communicate in this way you can exert your power quite astoundingly and it can be rather dominating. When you feel hard done by or concerned by someone's pattern of behaviour this can feel like a most wonderful weapon. Not for a moment am I suggesting that you dominate everyone in your life or become passive aggressive but *sometimes* a situation calls for such behaviour in order that the relationships that are woven into your life remain balanced and healthy. We cannot be nice all of the time if those in our life are not being pleasant in the first instance. Your life experience is too precious to have someone waltz their way through it with little concern or consideration for you and your loved ones. If the predicament so requires, you must stand up for yourself and those you care about.

Silence can have the impact that words cannot. The silence, particularly if there are few non-verbal cues, can leave the recipient quite mystified. If you relax your body posture and keep fairly still, and avert your gaze so that the other person cannot read your eye signals either, the other party can be left wondering what you are thinking and this can be intoxicating for you. You can sense the other person feeling dumbfounded and this can result in them really searching inwardly for clues as looking outwardly towards you for clues is revealing nothing. This introspection can assist the person to understand, albeit over time, what they are saying or doing wrong in their relationship with you. You needn't always verbalise where they are going wrong. In fact, if they realise for themselves they will tend to amend any such behaviour with much more gusto than if told by somebody else that something needs to change.

If you remove your verbal and non-verbal communication almost completely and simply use silence coupled with a look in the eyes this can often be sufficient to convey your message. Again, always remember the saying "the eyes are the window to the soul". It can be very easy to read eye signals to see if a person is being sincere, lying, feeling embarrassed, feeling proud and so on. When dealing with undesirable behaviour your response of silence coupled with eye contact can mean a number of things. There is no technique as such that one can employ in order to convey a certain emotion through their eyes other than *actually feeling* whatever it is that they wish to convey. Whether you are feeling sad, angry, offended, dismissive, despondent, fed up, happy, loving, or whatever it may be, your eyes will tell all as you genuinely *feel* the emotion.

If you let your silence and non-verbal communication do some of the talking for you instead of your mouth, you can successfully affect change in someone's behaviour. It will also allow you to communicate yourself better. Improving your relationships in this way can invite respect. It can also reduce the risk of unnecessary tension and disagreements.

Action Point -
Over the next few weeks identify three opportunities for using silence as a response to someone's undesirable behaviour. This could be someone being rude when they communicate with you, someone lying to you, or whatever it is that you do not like about the way someone behaves

with you or around you. On these occasions use the power of silence coupled with non-verbal communication to demonstrate your thoughts with the aim of affecting change.

Document your experiences on paper:

- why the three situations called for this response,
- how you felt when you used these techniques,
- how you felt afterwards at intervals of hours and days after the event,
- and what results have you achieved by doing so.

The results you achieve will either be:

a) a feeling of empowerment that you gain
b) or the change you affected in the other person's behaviour
c) or both.

Continue to utilise this new found knowledge in order to communicate better with others.

Chapter 16

I'm Not Psychic!

"Communication is a skill that you can learn. It's like riding a bicycle or typing. If you're willing to work at it, you can rapidly improve the quality of every part of your life."

- Brian Tracy

We've all been there. Feeling hard done by, wondering why the other person treats us the way they do and then overreacting in our response to it. Of course, it's easy to get carried away in our own minds thinking about how *we* feel.

Relationships are built on a foundation of each person's thoughts, emotions and actions. We all bring into our relationships old experiences that we have had and the meanings we have attached to them. Such experiences will inform our interpretation of who we are in our current relationships as well as whom we expect the other person to be. For example, if one has had negative experiences with a previous lover one might expect the new partner to behave similarly. It can take time to shrug off old memories and look at the new partner with new, fresh eyes. Similarly, if a previous relationship has created self-doubt or self-loathing these feelings can spill into new relationships.

Each relationship deserves to be judged on its own merits. In order to do so fairly you must look at the relationship through the other person's point of view as well as your own. By so doing you ensure you always get two sides of a story. Whether, for example, you are mediating between two family members or trying to understand the relationship between yourself and someone else, seeing the world through the eyes of all those concerned is vital.

In order to understand the other person's perception, and to open their eyes to yours, you need to open communication. Talk frankly. Voice your concerns and voice your desires. Encourage the other person to do the same. Assuming neither of you are psychic, one of you may not be as self-aware or otherwise aware of challenges and concerns as the other person in the relationship. You need to give each other a helping hand and the only way to do this is through open, honest communication. Don't make assumptions about what the other person knows or understands. Instead of arguing with someone when they do something that displeases you, simply let them know that this is so and invite similar communication from the other person too.

Although not always possible, it can be helpful to speak to a person about their behaviour that you do not like when you are both calm and at a time when the behaviour is not taking place. This method can often work better than spitting your comments at them when you are riled up. Even if you are telling the person in a calm manner you may embarrass the person if you speak of the behaviour immediately after it has occurred. This embarrassment may lead to defensiveness which can lead to arguments rather than acknowledgments. If they feel you are maturely communicating something to them that will strengthen your relationship, they will likely change their behaviour as requested.

Case Study -
Ever the energetic person who always wakes up in a good mood "Jemima" used to have a bad habit of bombarding her husband, "Tom", with questions, comments and things to do first thing as he awoke. Of course, Jemima was looking at the world through her eyes. When she did so, Tom would get incredibly mad at her for not giving him space and time to wake up. He would be grumpy and they would end up arguing at the very beginning of their day. You can imagine how terribly annoying Jemima found that but what she didn't realise was how terribly annoying Tom found her when she kept chattering on!

Jemima was completely oblivious to what she was doing wrong in Tom's eyes and each time he responded in this moody manner she wondered why on earth he was treating her this way. The first time he eventually told her what was wrong with her approach he did so whilst shouting at her in the heat of the moment, immediately after their altercation first thing in the morning. Now of course his "issue" with Jemima made perfect sense yet she was simply too offended by his seemingly hurtful behaviour to what seemed to Jemima to be her very reasonable behaviour. As a result, she found herself arguing back with him even though what he was saying made perfect sense.

Clearly she had not understood what he was inadvertently requesting as they continued to have this very same quarrel on a few further occasions. Only when they eventually had a discussion at a completely disassociated moment in time when they were both relaxed did Jemima fully comprehend his point of view. Tom simply wanted some peace and quiet when he awoke so that he could gear up for the day. Her ramblings in the morning were simply disrupting this process of his and really irritated him. He also now understood why she behaved in this way - because she awoke in a state of upbeat readiness for the day. Jemima never repeated this mistake again.

If you better pick your moments to communicate your feelings and needs you will have the same discussion fewer times and be faced with far less hostility. As a by product not only will you achieve the desired outcome much quicker and easier but you will also perceive the relationship as a much healthier one. You will feel understood and worthy and that in turn feeds how your future feelings for, and communications with, the other person will be shaped.

Remember the cycle of thoughts, feelings, actions and results that goes round and round? The way you communicate will either create a positive cycle of communication between you or a negative one and whatever form the cycle takes will colour your views of one another. It is imperative to realise that whilst the cycle may be a negative one and that may be because *you* have steered it this way, you will still associate the negative feelings with the *other* person although *you* may be entirely responsible for the negativity. You may go on to blame the other person; you may grow distant from them as a result. However, if the negativity was solely created by you then you will steadily destroy this relationship and repeat this pattern with the others in your life, now and in the future, over and over and over again. If you are creating the negativity even partially then *you* need to break the cycle. When you change your contribution to the cycle this will affect change in the way the other person perceives and behaves with you.

In some relationships trying to have open frank communication can be far more difficult than in the aforementioned anecdote. After many years or even a lifetime of inability to communicate candidly with one another, one is not going to turn this around over night. However, it is possible to work towards a relationship of honest communication as time goes by.

Case Study ----------------------------------
I love my father with all my heart. He was once fairly stern and growing up as children we found him pretty scary but he did also have his tender sides. As a man fighting to keep his five children on the straight and narrow, retain their cultural background despite being born in multi-cultural Britain, ensure they excelled in their education and grew up moralistic, polite, and respectful he was at times perceivably strict.

Like any good parent he simply wanted the best for his children. He had travelled a treacherous journey from Asia to a land of hope for the promise of a good standard of living for a family he would one day have. He had experienced *extremely* tough times in his early years in Britain in the 1960s, working incredibly hard to earn an honest living.

Once I had reached my late twenties he told me stories of his trials and tribulations. He one day recalled a time when he used to live with about seven other immigrants in a house with only two bedrooms to share between them.

This story was simply one of many stories he could have shared of the tough times he had experienced, all with that glimmer of hope that he would one day create a comfortable life for himself and his future family. He and his wife (my mother), when she came along, experienced many hardships for many, many years.

Due to the sheer fight for a good life that my parents endured, my father had absolutely no intention of letting us throw away the chance he and my mother had given us of success in our careers and personal lives.

Unfortunately, my father wasn't quite adept at open communication. As a result he felt frustrated that his children did not understand him or his good intentions and we did not really understand why he was so incredibly strict and "scary".

I did not learn of their tough times until I was much older, and sadly this was only one of the many things my father had not communicated to his children during their lifetime. The result was that his children misunderstood him and he himself felt very misunderstood indeed. Unfortunately this led to a breakdown in his relationships with his children. Whilst I too was affected by a lack of understanding I will always say that I have forever had a good relationship with my father. The reason: I've always remembered the good times and I've always remembered even the smallest tokens of love that he showed in the ways he could.

Whenever I attempted cooking at school he would eat the entire dish and claim it tasted great even though the other family members would refuse to eat it because in reality it was rather unappetising. He would take us out for wonderful day trips and clearly try his hardest to make every minute as fun-filled and enjoyable as possible. He would bring little treats home every so often for each child and he would offer to buy us the best item in the shop if that was what we wanted because that was his way of saying, "I love you, I want the best for you and I want to make you happy." The smallest things spoke so loudly and I always remember those moments vividly because actions do speak louder than words *but* sometimes you still have to communicate with words and that was the ingredient my father was sometimes lacking.

As I reached adulthood I found myself engaging my father in more stories about himself. This was borne out of my love for him and my curiosity about his life. When we are younger we can take life and people for granted. As we grow older we become increasingly aware of mortality and simultaneously develop a desire to work towards deeper, more meaningful relationships. I wanted to develop just such a relationship with my beloved father.

When we were sat alone he would be much more relaxed. He knew that we had always had a good relationship (for the most part) and he recognised that I was reaching out to him with my questions about him and his life. These factors created a loving, relaxed environment for him. As he spoke, I acknowledged his feelings and the misunderstandings that had taken place over the years between himself and his family. As I verbally communicated my acknowledgement of the misunderstandings and my recognition of his emotions spanning many decades of his life he clearly found the experience cathartic. He felt understood, finally. He felt heard and he felt better able to communicate. This became quite evident over the passing weeks and months.

The amazing thing is that such a profound difference took effect over just a few meetings of our minds. From then on everything changed. My father became more comfortable in his own skin, so to speak. He would enjoy off-loading to me and I felt great to be able to provide him with a space where he could talk about some of the things on his mind, share his burdens as well as his insights. Naturally, I reciprocated. I spoke to him about the things that were troubling me. I was honest about things that I previously would have been way too frightened to divulge to my father. We had always had a tight bond but it had now progressed to a new level.

My relationship with my father was closer than it had ever been and I now felt that, no matter what, we would always be close whereas I had wondered in my younger days whether we would drift apart through our inability to truly communicate with one another. That thought had burdened me for a while. Subconsciously the idea of not having a good relationship with my father for the rest of our time together tapped my brain into *fight-for-this-relationship* mode. There was no way that could be an option. I had gone from feeling bewildered by such thoughts to a *failure is not an option* mentality. As the saying goes, "when the dream's big enough, the facts don't count." The dream was, of course, big enough. The facts didn't count. I found a way.

What I hadn't anticipated was the secondary effect that our opened lines of communication and subsequent understanding relationship would have on the rest of the family. Although my father was now able to communicate with myself better his new found communication skills had not yet spilled over into his life with his other children. I decided that if he could not, I would. My new found awareness regarding my misunderstood father now urged me to speak on his behalf whenever necessary. I simply wanted to project my father and his intentions as they truly were so as to eradicate the false impressions that had been held for so many years.

Over time his other children began to see him in a different light too. This was partially due to the fact that he was now a much more relaxed person but by representing my father in a different light the others also began to see his unchanged ways differently. They began to understand him better. I certainly understood how the others had misunderstood him; we all had to a differing extent. As the weeks, months and years went by the family unit as a whole became closer and closer. Yes events occurred that helped both my father and his other children gain a shift in perspective but without the foundation of growing harmony and understanding that was already in place the family unit would not have gelled together as easily or as rapidly as it did.

The moral of the story? Communication is crucial. Communication is absolutely necessary for strong, loving, healthy relationships to be cultivated. One can only imagine how past relationships in one's life could have panned out better had one communicated better. However, one can proactively change how one communicates in the present so that all current and future relationships do become massively successful.

The small actions my father took demonstrated his love. We are thus reminded that actions speak louder than words even though words are also required for absolute success in communication.

In an earlier chapter we looked at how we speak to others non-verbally. This story reminds us that communication is a two way process and, therefore, we not only communicate our inner thoughts and intentions with our body language, we are also responsible for reading those of others.

If we miss the non-verbal signs and actions of someone's compassion, we may miss the opportunity to have a rewarding relationship with them. If you care enough about someone you owe it to them and yourselves to search hard for the signs of true love. It may be that the signs are buried deep within. Not everyone shows love in the same way and not everyone is adept at showing love.

Some people's feelings have been damaged in some way and they can sometimes be perceived as unlikeable characters when in reality they are just burdened with previous hurts. This can create defensiveness and insecurity in them.

When people do not feel comfortable within themselves they can engage with others in a less than effective way. They will often be searching for acceptance from others yet if they are not able to accept themselves for whom they are then others will struggle to accept them. Their inability to accept themselves can also result in a difficulty to accept others and this can lead to complications when relating to others.

As I asked my father about his life, his youth, his early adulthood, he recognised that I cared for him. We only consistently show an interest in someone's personal life, past and present, if we really care for that person and wish to build a relationship with them. By signalling my love and my desire to know him better my father became open and relaxed. This is where we began entering a more advanced phase of our relationship.

I felt that my father had been somewhat hard done by and set about trying to defend him. I put his case forward at every opportunity as I knew he was not yet always able to do so. As the others accepted more of him via the new perspective I was conveying on his behalf, both parties (my father and his other children) began to move closer towards one another. My father began to open up more and communicate better than he had ever done. His children began to understand him better. As the children began to understand him better, he began to communicate better. The positive effect bounced back and forth and it all began with better communication.

If you know that someone is no good at communicating, help them. Help them to communicate better with yourself and others. Ask them questions. Show a sincere interest in what they have to say. Really listen to and dig under the surface meanings to understand the feelings that lie beneath them. When you pick up on the underlying feelings you'll be surprised at how much you can affect a person positively by showing them that you have *truly* heard what they have said. It is only by acknowledging what someone is feeling deep down that you truly acknowledge the person within the exterior of the human body. When you shrewdly acknowledge the person within you will help them to relax and open up. The more they open up the better you will understand them, how they think and feel, their likes and dislikes, their interests and their values. As they relax and open up you will be able to build a meaningful relationship with them. We mustn't dismiss or pre-judge someone just because we haven't dug deep yet to find out whom they really are.

You do need to practice patience in getting to know somebody. How long you are willing to wait patiently for the relationship you desire with any given person is your personal choice. It will normally be determined by how much you love them and how desperate you are to make the relationship work. If it is a partner that you are now struggling to see a future with you may find your patience wearing thin but if you know that you absolutely want to keep this partner in your life forever then you will approach the situation with more gusto. If you are feeling impatient perhaps it is a sign of a deeper shift within your heart and mind that you need to acknowledge. Perhaps it is a sign that you see an ending point in the relationship. If you find yourself constantly fighting on, ask yourself if that is because you wish to make the relationship work whatever happens. Once you know what it is that you are aiming towards you will be able to reach your desired outcome much faster. Like anything, without a specific goal the actions required to get there will remain elusive.

You never know how long you have left with the people you care about. If you are reading this book you have clearly decided that you want things to change. Don't waste your time procrastinating. Start communicating in every way. Time is something we never get back. It is a most precious thing, it cannot be replenished.

You sometimes have to remind people or be reminded that everybody is different. You need to understand the world through their eyes so that you can build a more harmonious relationship. Help them to see your world through your eyes too. Perhaps they are missing some crucial information that will help them to bond better with you. Explain what the other person's actions mean and how they make you feel and give solid examples. Sometimes you may need to wait until examples have accumulated so that you can put your case forward. Whatever it takes, communicate openly and honestly in a constructive way.

Study your subject, be they your partner, friend, parent, child or yourself. Study and reflect. Reflect and evaluate. Evaluate and understand. When you understand your subject you will understand how to work with them, communicate with them, live with them, approach them, and get what you want from them whilst at the same time giving them what they want.

Action Point ----------------------------------
Write a list of three things you could ask the person you wish to communicate better with in order to build a stronger relationship. Come up with questions that invite the person to open up about deeper aspects of their being. You might ask about their childhood, their relationship with their parents or their old friends.

You'll be surprised at how easy it can be to keep the conversation going as more questions spring to mind based on their responses. You may also find similarities within your own life that you can talk about with them.

Now ask the person the questions you have come up with. Listen to their answers and dig deep into the underlying feelings and emotions that they are conveying in their responses. Relay your understanding to them to show them you have actively listened to what they have told you.

Repeat this every week or at least every fortnight when there are no outside interruptions and just the two of you are present.

As the weeks and months go by you will notice an improvement in your relationship. Write down your findings.

The barriers will come down, the mutual understanding will increase and the relationship will grow. All it takes is a few questions to get the ball rolling.

Chapter 17
Why Didn't I Realise Sooner?

"Wisdom consists of the anticipation of consequences."

- Norman Cousins

Some believe they are invincible. That no matter what they say or do, they will come out unscathed. That they can go through life without fear of repercussions. Well that simply is not true. There are always consequences.

Every decision you make has consequences. Every action you take has consequences. Even every thought you think has consequences. These consequences affect your life and your relationships. They affect how people you have relationships with perceive you, how you perceive them *and* how you perceive yourself in relationships. The effects can be felt immediately or after some time and you may not even realise the consequences you have set into motion until it's too late.

If you treat someone less than respectfully and fail to demonstrate that you care for them, there will be a breakdown of the relationship. If you lie to someone all the time they will begin to distrust you. If you frequently humiliate someone in front of others they will begin to despise you. If you show a lack of interest in someone's life and in the person himself, he will begin to drift away from you. Simple, right? Yes and no.

Whilst this all seems very obvious and the things you do can clearly be damaging your relationships you may not recognise them as such when it is happening. It can be that the other party does not consciously recognise the effects of your behaviour either. This is why people veer off the course of happiness in their relationships without realising what it is that has taken them off track. They're left with the resulting feelings and consequences but don't necessarily realise what caused the misdirection.

On noticing the problems a person may try to fix the resulting issues rather than the root cause. Unfortunately this can be seen in modern day medicine whereby symptoms are treated rather than the underlying problem. The result is that the illness itself can reoccur or it may never go away in the first place. This illness may also lead on to further health implications. Similarly, if you try to mend your relationship problems on the surface you may never get to the root cause and actually repair what it is that has caused your current problem and this may then lead to further relationship health implications.

Case Study ----------------------------------

A lady named "Grace" fell in love with a man named "Dean". When Grace and Dean met, their personalities complemented one another's and they had much fun together. They shared many interests and those that they did not share they made an effort to accommodate.

As the years went by Grace began to recognise that Dean was quite an introverted personality type whilst she was not. This led to Grace accommodating Dean's desires more and more out of sheer love for him, as well as a feeling that she did not wish to fight for a sociable night out. She felt that it was difficult to persuade him into doing the things that she wanted to do and so more often than not she would take what seemed like the easier option of simply doing what he liked to do. After all, it wasn't as though she didn't enjoy those things too. So long as she was spending time with her beloved she was happy, as was Dean, and that was all that mattered.

Only did it hit Grace after a number of years that the life she and Dean had created for themselves was a life that catered much more to his desires than to both of their needs. In the weeks and months after the onset of this realisation she began to feel upset and bitter towards Dean. She was upset about the fact that her life no longer resembled the lifestyle she had imagined for herself nor one that met *her* needs. She felt upset that getting Dean to do the things that she wanted to do was such an uphill struggle. She felt as though she was being taken for granted and not appreciated nearly enough as she felt she deserved. She became unhappy and developed feelings of resentment towards Dean.

"The strange thing is," Grace recalls, "I didn't completely realise what was creating a divide in our relationship, why we were starting to lose that special closeness and why I had started feeling bitter and almost indifferent towards Dean. I didn't feel special anymore. I felt ignored."

As the months went by the pieces of the puzzle came together. As Grace evaluated all that had been happening over the latter years of their relationship she realised that something drastically needed to change. She also began to identify the fact that they had both played their part in what was, in Grace's mind, a breakdown of their relationship.

Grace had neglected her own needs as much as Dean had done so. *She* was the one that had made the decision to accommodate his needs over and above her own for so long. *She* was the one that had decided that it was easier to do as Dean wanted than to fight for her own desires. *She* was the one who had allowed this pattern to continue for so long. She had begun to feel resentful towards Dean and whilst Dean had certainly played his part in behaving as though oblivious to Grace's needs, *she* had failed to stand up for herself and simply say, "I need to realise my own goals of living a sociable, activity filled life and you need to be a part of that." *She* had reinforced his bad, ignorant, self-centred behaviour by accommodating rather than objecting to it and so *she* needed to turn this around with a new response to what was happening in their relationship.

Upon noting the part she had played in her unhappiness, and although still angry at Dean for his lack of thoughtfulness, she set about making changes. One of the methods she utilised was having a handful of arguments with him regarding the issue over the space of a few months. She found opportunities, no matter how small, to draw attention to her plight. She let him know repeatedly how she felt, how she perceived his lack of consideration for her, how she felt disregarded and somewhat unloved. She let him know that he could not take their relationship for granted. She highlighted that having a relationship and having a tremendously happy, incredibly loving relationship were two different things. That there were two paths and it was up to him to decide which path he wanted. A third path that led to life apart was never an option in their minds leaving solely two paths for him to choose from.

Grace also conveyed her desire for drastic change by pulling Dean up on his behaviour each time he fell into old habits. When he would not see the situation through Grace's eyes she would remind him of her needs. He knew from their discussions that he needed to show he cared by accommodating her needs. He now knew that by not honouring his commitment to make her happy he was not worthy of her love. By Grace demanding he not forget her needs she reinforced the notion that she was important and that his dismissal of her requirements was not acceptable. She asserted her value as a person and this will have reminded Dean of the value of having a happy Grace in his life.

Grace also acknowledged that she had perhaps placed 75 per cent of her needs for socialising upon Dean whereas a lower percentage was far more reasonable. After all, one cannot expect one person to cater for such a large portion of one's need for a social life. Upon noting this she steadily reintroduced herself to the world of socialising in a way that she had done in the past. This meant that Dean was relieved of some of the pressure to fulfil Grace's needs. What this also meant was that Grace felt much happier within her relationship with Dean and fully appreciated the times he undertook sociable activities with her.

The release of anger, Dean's *and* Grace's acknowledgement of Grace's needs, the reduction in dissatisfaction with the relationship and the happier life experience that Grace was having resulted in a better relationship experience for both of them. Consequently, they began to appreciate each other more. Their refined conduct within their relationship positively fed their cycle of thoughts, feelings, behaviour and results. They became happier and stronger as a couple as a result of the clarity on what they both needed and expected from their relationship coupled with the actions taken to make the necessary changes.

This story exemplifies some of the lessons we have been exploring thus far. First of all let us note that Grace had allowed Dean to treat her in a way that she had not found considerate. Whilst he too was at fault as he should have had a greater inclination to do more of the things that she desired, Grace had owned the fact that she had reinforced Dean's rather self-focused behaviour. This is important as if you continue to blame someone else entirely for something that isn't going the way you'd hoped then you are essentially absolving yourself of all responsibility. Of course, if you want things to change in your relationships, and life, then you must honour your responsibility. Besides, this is the only factor that you have 100 per cent control over so it only makes sense to manipulate this aspect to your own advantage. Only when you take full responsibility for the shaping of your relationships, and life, will you reap the benefits of creating the experiences you desire.

Not only had Grace reinforced Dean's behaviour, she had also failed to take a stand for what she wanted. She had chosen to take what she had mistakenly thought was the easy route by not fighting for her needs and instead spending time with Dean in the ways that fit his personality. She thought that the battle of convincing him to do what she wanted would expend greater effort than doing the things that he wanted. Ironically, the ensuing months and years of doing the things he wanted took their toll on their relationship which actually became the bigger price to pay. In other words, by following what she deemed an easier path to happiness she inadvertently took on the more challenging path to happiness. She reached happiness eventually but she paid a higher price to get there. The consequences of her actions became clear long after she had made her choices.

There are always consequences and sometimes it is easy to think that the seemingly simple path is the less arduous one whereas it is actually the other. Whilst hindsight is a wonderful thing one should look at what the lessons of one's own life, and those of others' lives, have taught one. One must also think one's actions through in advance by trying to anticipate what the outcomes of various actions might be over an extended period of time. Think of potential pitfalls. Think of the short, medium and long term consequences that may arise as a result of intended actions.

As you begin to consciously pay more attention to your life, your experiences and the experiences of others, you begin to become better able to **identify the paths that lead to good outcomes** when you have more than one option to follow. Experiences tell us a great deal about ourselves and our choices. Ask yourself if you tend to make good choices or bad choices. You will know the answer by the outcomes you have experienced.

Whether you tend to make good choices or bad choices you need to look for the patterns that stand out to you. For example, if you notice that you have made the choice to let people have their way in several relationships throughout your life and this has ultimately led to later problems in the relationships whereby they control your relationship more, then you need to recognise that this method is clearly not serving you well. By making different choices you can then determine the success of those altered changes.

Some altered actions take time to evidence the outcome but in some instances you can test the water with small altered actions that induce relatively quick outcomes. This can help you to either build your conviction in the new way you have chosen to relate to someone or establish if it too is counterproductive to the relationship's success. However, when employing such testing tactics you must be aware that you may come up against resistance from the other party and this does not always mean that it is not the best way for you to progress your relationship towards a more mutually beneficial experience. It may simply be a case of short-term discomfort for them, and possibly you, before you *both* reap the rewards of a more mutually fulfilling relationship.

Imagine if Grace had attempted to persuade Dean into doing more of the sociable activities that suited her personality and needs in the earlier years of their relationship. Based on what Grace had experienced she would have been confronted with Dean's resilience and it would have felt like a struggle. If she had stood her ground firmly at that time it could have taken a few short months or even just a few weeks of persisting with this plan of action for Grace to reap the benefits of her approach. She would have discovered far, far sooner that she and Dean could both have the relationship experience they wanted by evenly splitting their sociable time together between the things that they both enjoyed doing. She would then not have paid the consequences of discontentment, feelings of being unloved, dismissed and thoughts of bitterness towards Dean. At the end of the day, if for a few weeks or months you test a new approach to a testing situation in your relationship, you may come up against reluctance, arguments, anger and other difficulties, but this does not mean it does not work. Whether it works or does not, at least you have only spent a short period of time seeing if it is the right path towards a fantastic relationship experience. If it is not you have not wasted years following a disastrous path as Grace did. If it is, then you have proactively created that rewarding relationship.

If you remember, Grace also took the decision to remind Dean of their discussions about the need for change in their relationship each time he fell into his old habits again. There were two ways Grace could have handled this. One would have been to essentially give in and stop fighting (in the face of Dean's reluctance) for what she needed *and* what their relationship ultimately needed. The other would have been to fight for her socialising needs. As with anything in life, each path led to consequences. Had she given in she would have worsened her situation. She would have again reinforced Dean's self-centred behaviour. She would have also reinforced her lack of worth in her own mind as well as in Dean's. This would then have fed future problems in her self-confidence as well as in their relationship. Instead she chose to fight on which led to the consequence of Dean progressively improving his behaviour, thus creating a much stronger, happier relationship.

The third thing that Grace changed was the way that she approached her socialising needs. She had previously expected Dean to fulfil these needs to a huge extent. She then realised the imbalance that was being created by her lack of effort to socialise with others as well. This new awareness and altered approach led to a consequence of less pressure on Dean which meant that whatever they did do together socially was far more appreciated by Grace. With this more fairly balanced approach Dean's socialising commitment quotient was lower and, therefore, easier to achieve. The socialising Grace did away from Dean also satisfied her desires more and she thus felt happier which undoubtedly had the consequence of a positive knock-on effect on their relationship.

What started off as one problem created out of one bad choice - failing to acknowledge and satisfy her own needs - Grace created a sad state of affairs. Do you see how one decision to take what appears to be the easy way out can lead to more problems than one might have *ever* imagined? For one's own benefit, one should always use one's previous experiences to learn how to move through life in a more rewarding way. Fortunately for Grace, once she had awoken to the root cause of her relationship dissatisfaction, she remembered this life lesson and continued to remind Dean of it, rather than allowing herself and Dean to fall back into old habits. Had she not, who knows how far her relationship with Dean would have unravelled.

There are *always* consequences to everything you do, be they negative or positive. When you hit bumps in the road of your relationship you need to step back and acknowledge something is not right. You must then search for the reasons. What actions have you taken that have resulted in these consequences? You will need to glance as far back as necessary. You then need to take responsibility for the part you play. Remember, in relationships there is *always* a part you play. Once you have identified the actions that have resulted in the negative outcomes, look for ways to amend your actions in order that you produce different results. Be persistent in maintaining the new, improved course of action. Do not falter from it or you'll be slipping back to discontentment. Remember why you changed your approach to your relationship and then see your intended changes through to the end, even when it feels easier to not do so. Remember, what feels easier may not be easier in the long run and what feels happier may create far greater unhappiness in the long term.

Look to the future to foresee, to the best of your ability, how your actions and those of others concerned will impact on your relationship in the short, medium and long term. This is not difficult to do it's just that it's easy to forget that one should. **Your mind should be actively involved in creating the current and future experiences that you want. You cannot create happy, healthy relationships on auto-pilot.** By being thoughtful, thankful and taking persistent positive action you can create the relationships that you desire.

Action Point ----------------------------------
Identify any challenges/problems you are experiencing in the relationship(s) that you are seeking to remedy. Write these down on paper.

Next, write down what success will look, feel and sound like when you are relieved of these issues.

For each challenge/problem write down what you are doing or have been doing for some time that has led to this issue.

Lastly, write down how you intend to change your behaviour in order to resolve the problems. For example:

Problem

I feel like I am constantly being made to feel insignificant.

Goal

I would like to feel and be seen as important by my partner and family. I want them to hear them say, "I don't know how we'd cope without you."

Reasons For Problem

I have not focused on my own career as much as I should have.

My partner puts my needs second to his needs or the family needs - because I let him.

I have always let other people dictate what I should achieve.

Solutions To Help Me Achieve My Goal

I will decide what type of career I want and then take the necessary steps to achieve it, whether that be studying part-time or getting some work experience or teaching myself with free information from the internet.

I will assert my needs more to my husband and family. I will fairly balance their needs with mine. I will let them know I am important too and my needs must also be met.

I will stand up for my career choices and follow my heart rather than simply do what other people expect me to do.

Once you have completed the above be sure to set yourself some simple SMART goals that help you to achieve your said goals, and then stick to them. See Appendix for information on how to set simple, effective SMART goals.

Chapter 18

Relationships And Attraction - The Other Kind

"The greatest discovery of my generation is that human beings can alter their lives by altering their attitudes of mind."

- William James

After the documentary entitled *The Secret* hit the stores the world truly awoke to a theory that is usually referred to as the law of attraction. It is not that this film, or the book by Rhonda Byrne that it was adapted from, was the first informative account of its kind. It had merely been explained in such simple terms that word spread from person to person. Classic bestsellers, such as Napoleon Hill's groundbreaking book *Think and Grow Rich* also discussed the law of attraction theory, albeit in different terms. *The Secret*, however, introduced the theory to a wider audience with its more easily digestible explanation. From then on it seems people have popped up all over the world trying to help others to grasp the theory and explain how to implement it. Even a whole variety of professionals have integrated the theory into their way of thinking and working. Whether you believe in the law of attraction or believe it is all nonsense there are definitely some aspects of the theory which most people would agree upon.

The theory is based on the premise that "like attracts like". It suggests that your predominant thoughts, when believed with absolute conviction, will manifest into their physical counterparts within your life. Napoleon Hill's famous quote, "What the mind of man can conceive and believe, it can achieve", is just another way of describing how the theory works in practice. Those who have achieved greatness, for example, in business or within the realms of charitable work, will often prescribe to this very notion that they had begun with a clear vision of what they wanted, they wholeheartedly believed it possible and they subsequently achieved it.

Some will say that you need a positive mental attitude to achieve what you want in life whilst at the same time refuting the law of attraction theory. Surely the two are interlinked, are they not? To have a positive mental attitude is to view your world through optimistic thought processes. A positive mental attitude allows you to obtain success in your career, relationships, physical health, or whatever it is, by adopting positive thoughts, emotions and behaviours that are conducive to achieving a desired outcome. It also means positively evaluating things that have happened and things that one expects to happen. By so doing people believe they will achieve that which they desire and positively expect. The law of attraction theory would similarly state that if you mentally focus on that which you positively expect you would attract that which you positively expect. In both cases, whether you were to say you were implementing a positive mental attitude or the law of attraction, as a result you would find yourself thinking, feeling, behaving and evaluating in a way that was conducive to achieving your desires. In both cases the thought process would be the instigator. In both cases there are proponents and opponents of the theory. However, if you want to change your relationships, and life, for the better then is it worthwhile adopting some basic principles that thousands of extremely successful people claim are vital? What have you got to lose by adopting these principles into your own life? That's right, nothing.

Take a look at these basic principles:

- Like attracts like.
- You attract into your life a response to your own outward behaviour.
- You attract into your life a manifestation of your thoughts.
- You attract into your life, at your own free will.

You don't have to subscribe to the law of attraction theory or any theory for that matter in order to appreciate that the above principles are true. Let's have a look at some really basic examples of each.

Like attracts like. Your friends are similar to you in some way or another. Sometimes you have different types of friends that serve to tantalise the different aspects of your personality. One friend might appeal to your sociable side whilst another may appeal to the feminine or masculine side of your personality.

You attract into your life a response to your own outward behaviour. If you behave in a way that is aggressive, you are likely to receive an aggressive response back. If you are rude with someone they will likely be rude back. You will get back what you give out. If you behave in a way that is gentle and loving you are likely to receive a gentle, loving response back. However you behave will attract a response of some sort and that response is likely to be similar to the way you have behaved.

You attract into your life a manifestation of your thoughts. The law of attraction theory states that you can attract any objects, experiences and people into your life, no matter how big or small, if you focus on them and believe with unshakeable conviction that you can have those things. If you struggle to believe this to be true let's break it down using some simple examples.

When you feel yourself coming down with a cold or cough you can do one of two things. You can focus on it and expect it to happen or you can focus on it not happening and expect it to not happen. Whichever thought path you choose (you will become ill or you won't become ill) will be followed by certain actions that you will take consciously and/or subconsciously, actions that are either conducive to becoming ill in this way or conducive to not becoming ill in this way. The end result will tend to be a match for what you are expecting, perhaps because you took certain actions which acted as a catalyst for your expectation to become a reality. That certainly makes sense, doesn't it?

Another more common example will be a person who tells himself and the rest of the world that he is bad at remembering peoples' names. Imagine you are such a person. If you frequently tell yourself this and mentally succumb to this "fact" as though you are helpless to change it you will behave accordingly. You will not normally do your utmost to remember the name of someone you have just met as you have already failed in your mind before you have even tried due to your self-belief that you have some sort of innate inability to memorise peoples' names. When you then do not remember the person's name you will see it as proof of your self-belief and it thus becomes a self-fulfilling prophecy. You would then repeat this cycle over and over again, each time adding support to your hypothesis. The fact is, however, that your *lack of effort* in trying to memorise the name will have impacted your ability to memorise it much more so than some imagined inability.

If you told yourself you *are* good at remembering names you would take the appropriate actions to memorise the name of each new person you met. You would utilise some sort of technique for memorising it. This could be as simple as silently repeating it five times to yourself when you are first introduced to a new person. Thus the names would become consolidated within the memory and less likely to be forgotten than by someone who makes little active effort to remember it purely because they have told themselves that they cannot.

Furthermore, someone who does not agree with the law of attraction theory may not agree that something appears to have manifested as a result of purposely attracting it. However, they can still agree with the fact that one may simply be able to identify when something has manifested rather than failing to.

When you expect something negative to come out of a situation it is easy to identify the negatives more clearly (as that is what you are focused on) and to overlook the positives. For example, if you are meeting someone in a car park and they say they will be arriving in a red car you will be on the lookout for a red car. Now if they end up arriving in a blue car you would still be searching for them in a red car as that is your focus and expectation. Similarly, if you are expecting something negative to happen you will be focused on finding it. You could completely overlook the positive aspects as you are not expecting them and, therefore, not focusing on them. One might say that you attracted into your life a manifestation of your negative thoughts but if that idea doesn't sit right with you, you can at least believe that you:

a) behaved in a way that was conducive to the creation of your negative expectation, and
b) by focusing your mind on a negative expectation you identified the negative when it manifested.

In other words, the law of attraction theory states that you draw to yourself that which you think about whilst another way to understand this would be to say that you create and you notice that which happens because it matches what you think about. Either way, whether you believe you are *causing* something negative to happen with your *thoughts* or *are yourself causing and noticing* something negative that is happening, your focus is on the same thing, in this case, something negative. The bottom line is whatever you focus on will affect your relationships and life.

You attract into your life, at your own free will. Of course you do. You design your life. You create your world. You make the choices that attract the good, bad and the ugly into your life.

Now that we have a basic understanding of these terms of attraction, we can now explore further.

Like attracts like in terms of who you are as a person, how you think and how you behave. That's simple enough to understand but how often do you really consider this factor in your day to day interactions with others? We have touched upon some of this in previous chapters but let us now delve further into the effect you have on your relationships.

You want to attract likeable people into your life, right? Right. Then the first thing to address is whether or not you are likeable in order to attract others with that same characteristic into your life. Not whether you are likeable on the surface. People soon enough learn someone's true nature. Even if you think you are portraying a certain persona that which is underneath will come through and that is the part that needs to be likeable. If you are not likeable you will struggle to build long lasting relationships. If you do not believe yourself to be likeable then self-discovery will help you to understand why and change it for the better. By implementing some of the techniques learnt in this book and by enlisting the help of a relationship coach you can get to the bottom of why you are the way you are.

Discovering why you are not likeable and how you can genuinely change that will lead you towards greater life satisfaction because relationships lead to a fully rounded life experience. Even if you do not want a romantic partner or children it's still a good idea to have friends in your life if you want to enjoy life to its fullest.

If you believe yourself to be likeable, are you sure that is how others perceive you? Have you slowly turned into a less likeable version of yourself and not realised? This may sound silly but sometimes our experiences in life can slightly alter our way of being. If the changes take place in extremely small increments it can be difficult to detect. If you believe yourself to be somewhat unlikeable there will be underlying reasons for it. For example, some people become bitter as a result of difficult relationships they've had in the past and this can translate into a less than amiable disposition. Without acknowledging the underlying reasons for this you cannot fully solve the problem. You need to work on the root cause, not the symptoms. For a fundamental change to take place you need to address the root of the problem. So long as you believe that you were not simply born unlikeable, you made that change somewhere along the path of your life. Identify when in your mind you were likeable and when you feel you became unlikeable. You might find that you are able to identify that you had always felt amiable up until a certain point in your life and then some time lapsed after which, you notice with hindsight, you became less amiable. When you have identified such a period where the change appears to have taken place think about what was happening at that point in your life. You might identify the period as ranging between the age of "x" and the age of "y" or between the years "a" and "b" or between events "p" and "q". It is not only important to look at that particular phase of your life but it serves as the best starting point. You may need to work backwards if evaluating this period of your life brings little revelation. Working backwards can help you to peel the layers of what has happened and perhaps what is still happening. You might recall feeling a certain way. Working backwards you may associate that feeling to a number of incidents that occurred. Those incidents may have occurred because you had behaved in a certain way. You may have behaved in a certain way due to the way you had perceived a situation or a relationship. That situation or relationship may have sparked a negative feeling within you that changed the way you began to see yourself or the world or both, and so on. When fundamental changes take place within your being they do not tend to come about as a result of isolated incidences, they usually happen as part of a secondary effect and your task, as this is *your* life, is to unearth the pieces of that puzzle.

If like attracts like you need to become every bit the person you want to attract and keep in your life. If you want someone who is caring and forgiving then you will need to be caring and forgiving with others. For the longevity and happiness of a relationship there are certain fundamentals that must be adhered to by both parties. Therefore, you need to adopt them in order to attract others that adopt them *or* in order to attract others *into* adopting them. They are discussed in greater detail in Chapter 20 but for now they are namely:

- love,
- trust,
- respect,
- friendship
- communication and
- commitment.

Identify which of these principles, if any, you fail to espouse in the relationship that you intend to improve. Discover the root cause of your failure to adopt them and then set about making the necessary changes.

Don't go through life on autopilot. Think about what you are thinking, saying and doing. Only then can you proactively influence your world into delivering a desirable life experience.

Bearing in mind all that we have discussed in this chapter so far, the case study below is a great example of how people can forget that the world responds in likeness to how we think and behave, whether to our advantage or detriment.

Case Study -
A man named "Cameron" ran a small business from his office. He relished the idea of bossing people around and when he had enough staff members to look after the majority of the business he enjoyed letting people know what they should be doing and could be doing better.

Once he had employed a number of workers he became increasingly arrogant and began demotivating them with his aggressive approach. In his mind Cameron thought of the workforce as indebted to him for being paid a wage and this seeped through in his management style. He would patronise and belittle them publicly. More often than not he would be heard moaning about a lack of results from the sales force or about some other issue he had with the staff.

What he fantastically failed to realise was that he was at the helm and, therefore, the responsibility for the success or failure of the team ultimately rested on his shoulders. He created chaos that stemmed from his mind and filtered into the business and then complained about the chaos within the operation of the business. He created uncertainty with his ever-changing methods and direction and then blamed the workforce for lack of progress. Bit by bit he corroded the morale of the workforce.

Cameron was so caught up in satisfying his own desire to exert his power and control that he didn't even think about the response he would attract to his cruel behaviour. He lusted after money in such a way that he forgot the basic principles of morality. He thought mostly of his immediate gains and often forgot about the long term response.

Cameron would not only embarrass the staff members in front of their colleagues he would also sometimes fail to uphold his promises in relation to earnings. This created bitterness and uncertainty for the employees and they lost respect for Cameron and the organisation itself.

Cameron's maltreatment of his staff eventually led to a decline in morale, business sales and loyalty. Just as Cameron treated his staff with disregard, they began to treat his requests and his business with disregard. The productivity of the staff decreased because they no longer felt motivated to work for someone with such little compassion and because the bitterness towards Cameron grew. Each time he mistreated them another layer of dislike and bitterness enveloped the boss-employee relationship until one by one most of the employees had resigned.

Cameron was forever wasting huge amounts of time and money on hiring people to replace those he had hired and pushed away with his negative, nasty behaviour. He eventually had to begin playing a much more proactive role in the business too, something he had previously shied away from.

Cameron attracted into his life that which he had projected - anger and disregard. Cameron attracted into his life a response to his own outward behaviour - aggression, disrespect, disloyalty.

Cameron's true story is a very clear example of how the way he responded to the world around him affected how those concerned responded back. He thought he had the upper hand as the employer paying a wage. He failed to recognise that as employees his workforce could uproot and earn a wage elsewhere instead. Relationships have to be mutually beneficial or one party will uproot and simply move away from the unsatisfying relationship they are experiencing and even move towards having a satisfying relationship experience with someone else.

You control your thoughts. Earlier in the chapter we touched upon the fact that you attract into your life a manifestation of your thoughts. Whatever you focus your mind on is what you will consciously and subconsciously work towards. By focus I don't mean once in a while but, rather, frequently. This is why goal setting is so important. This is also why some people use affirmations to channel their thoughts towards the obtainment of their desires and believe in using positive self-talk and removing negative self-talk from their lives.

Whatever you fill your mind with will affect you in some way or another. Companies advertise their products and services on TV, the radio and the internet because they know that what you see and hear repeatedly will have an effect. If all advertising was banned we would make different choices about what to buy. Parents and teachers too mould children into thinking and behaving in a certain fashion by repeatedly teaching them about the world and life. As a result, the beliefs we grow up with and the things we learn to like and dislike often stem from that which we are taught by the media, parents, teachers, siblings, friends and society. Within thirty seconds we can usually identify several current beliefs that we hold that have come from our parents, let alone the rest of the influencers. Had you been brought up at a different time in a different place with a different family in a different culture, you would think differently. You would hold a different set of values and beliefs than the person you are today. So the question is what do you fill your mind with?

You are in charge of what you let in from the outside world and you have the ability to influence your own mind and heart.

Recent studies by Rollin McCraty and his colleagues at the Institute of HeartMath have shown that the heart plays a far greater role in our lives than we first realised. They found that **the heart actually influences decision making and influences the parts of the brain that are involved in cognition (e.g. memory), perception and emotional processing (feelings).** The heart sends signals to the brain via electromagnetic field interactions and thus influences the way the brain functions. The heart's magnetic field is approximately 5000 times stronger than the brain's magnetic field. The signals of the heart influence the entire body and can be detected several feet away. Such findings indicate that the heart is way more sophisticated and influential than we ever realised. Studies show that the heart has its own ability to remember, learn, and make decisions independently of the brain. Therefore, the heart is vital to achievement, understanding, mental health and relationships. So, going back to what I was saying, you are the gatekeeper of the external factors that positively and negatively influence your heart and mind.

In order to enjoy happy, fulfilling relationships with those important to you, you need to take control of what you let in. If you let others, society, media and influential people in your life, control your heart and mind then you will struggle to experience the relationships that you personally want to experience. We cannot simply live as others expect us to. We cannot have the types of relationships that others have with their parents, partners, children, friends, and colleagues because we are not them. If we allow ourselves to be controlled by external influences we become enslaved by them. If we allow ourselves to be controlled by other peoples' expectations for their own relationships and those of others, then we will not reach the pinnacle of happiness.

The first thing to establish is, as always, the goal - your goal. Your relationship goals are defined by what?

- What specifically do you want your relationship to bring?
- How do you want your relationship to make you feel about yourself and about the other party involved?
- How do you want the relationship to make you feel for the rest of your life?
- What words would you want the other party to use if asked to describe the way their relationship with you made them feel?
- What traits do you want the other person to possess?
- What types of experiences do you want the relationship to bring?
- What else do you want your relationship to bring?
- When do you want to achieve all of the above by?

Notice, the above asks you to think about what you do want, not what you don't want. You must always focus on what you do want because if you focus on what you do *not* want then you are still focusing your energy on it, aren't you? Always remember that whatever you focus on you will move towards. Therefore, always focus on your desires rather than fears. Whether you believe in the law of attraction or not, we can all agree upon the importance of focusing the mind on desirable, rather than undesirable, outcomes.

By now you should have defined your relationship goals more than once as a result of having completed the exercises within this book. There may well be a difference now in what you had originally perceived as your relationship goals and part of the purpose of asking you to write them out more than once was to show you that you evolve and so do your goals. Goals, like a business plan, are not set in stone. They are forever evolving as you follow the desires of your heart and mind. You always have goals within your heart and mind, it's whether you remember to clearly identify them and positively focus on them that will determine your success and speed in attaining them.

If you set out in the car to reach a destination but you only have a vague idea of the area rather than the specific address, will you find your destination? If you do find it, will you get there on time or will it take you a long time to find it and will you get there much later than you had desired? Will you spend more money than is necessary as you drive around using up more fuel whilst looking for the destination? Will you have to spend more money than required on an overnight hotel stay or pay for a few extra meals than anticipated in order to sustain you whilst you look for your vague destination? When you finally do get there, *if you even get there*, will you have made it there in time or will you have missed what you were going there for? Will you have wasted time, money and energy in trying to achieve something nebulous when you could have set out with the exact destination in mind?

If you have vague goals of any sort that are not clearly defined you will waste time, money and opportunities along your journey to reach them. The path you take may become so littered with distractions, waste and unnecessary stresses that you may never actually achieve your goals. You need to define your focus so that you are crystal clear in your mind as to what specifically you would like to achieve, when you want to achieve it by, and how you will feel when you have achieved it. If you can define your goals in as much detail as possible you can be sure that you will move towards them if you have a *real* desire to achieve them. If your desire is not a real desire then you will stop putting in the effort that is required and subsequently the goal will slip farther and farther away from your grasp.

Setting goals. They key questions to answer about any goal so that you may define it clearly are:

- What is the goal?
- What will success look like?
- What will success sound like?
- What will success feel like?
- When will you have achieved it by?

By answering these questions you first define the goal succinctly. You then elaborate on indicators that you have achieved the goal. You will know you have achieved success because you will become something or someone, you will see certain signs, you will feel particular emotions and you will have obtained certain achievements.

Imagine. It can be a useful exercise to first sit and relax with closed eyes in a peaceful place and imagine what your goals are. Whilst this technique can be applied to all goals we are in this instance looking at your relationship goals. When you find a relaxing, quiet place you feel calm and relaxed yourself. Soaking in a hot bath or sitting in the sun in the garden on a warm day can aid the relaxation of your mind and body. Imagine how you would ideally like your relationship to be.

When you commit to this exercise and once you have imagined your ideal relationship you will notice that deep down you do know what you specifically want out of your relationships with the people in your life. Defining it simply means taking the time to think about it in vivid detail.

Ask yourself how much difference there is between where you are now and where you want to be. You may notice that there are actually just a few tweaks required and on the other hand you may notice that there is quite a chasm to leap over. If the former is true then this perception will create a sense of relief and excitement that the journey to your ideal relationship needn't take too much effort or time. If the latter is true then you'll find it serves as a wake-up call as to how far off the course of happiness your relationship is. This new insight will raise awareness of the level of commitment now required if you wish to rescue and repair your relationship. How you approach this task will tell you how committed you are to achieving success. In other words, it will tell you how important it really is to you to fight for this relationship.

Commit your vision to writing. Once you have imagined your ideal relationship vividly you must then note down with pen and paper every detail you have conjured up. You then add to it a specific date by which you believe it is possible to achieve this ideal relationship by and would like to achieve it by. You have then committed your goal to memory and to paper.

It always feels much easier and takes less effort to achieve a goal that you are *really* excited about. Therefore, whatever you can do that creates excitement about a goal is very important and will massively help keep you motivated to achieve it. One way you can improve your motivation and ease of the journey, and keep your eye on the goal, is by utilising a goals poster.

Create your goals poster. This is simply a board or large sheet of thick paper that you attach images, or other representation, to in order to create a collage of your vision and reminders of your goal. This is a way of bringing your vision to life. You might add images of the types of restaurants you would like to eat out in together or a holiday destination that you would like to go to. It may be activities that you would like to enjoy together or a house that you would like to live in with someone. It may be the gifts you would like to give and receive or a family of your own that you might want to start. You can also add pictures that convey the emotions you would like to feel when in the company of that person, for example, joy, security or deep love.

When you put together your goals poster or vision board, or whatever you wish to call it, you should feel a sense of excitement when you look at it. If you don't then the pictures either do not convey your said goals *or* your goals aren't really your true goals *or* you don't believe in your ability to achieve them. If you don't believe in your ability to achieve them you never will. You cannot achieve something, other than by chance, if you do not believe you can. This is your life and happiness we are talking about and so you certainly wouldn't want to leave things up to chance, would you?

If you do not believe you can achieve them then you either set yourself unrealistic goals or goals that do not reflect your true desires. If the goals are unrealistic, why have you decided to set them? Can they be amended to make them more achievable? Is the time frame too unrealistic and perhaps needs extending? Are the goals themselves too unrealistic for you to find them believable at this moment in time? Whilst we often hear that we should reach for the stars there is little point in thinking about reaching for the loftiest heights if we don't really believe we can reach them. Reach for goals that are closer and when you've achieved those then set yourself a new goal to reach for that loftier place when it begins to feel achievable. Even if you believe you can achieve a fantastically huge goal it can still help to break your larger goal down into smaller goals that can be achieved sooner and easier. This makes the task in hand much easier and each time you achieve another goal you positively feed your thoughts about the master goal itself and your self-confidence.

If you have set yourself goals that you cannot get excited about, even once you have ensured that they are broken down and feel achievable, then something is not right. Have you only set those goals because you think you should or because others dictate you should? Alternatively, have you simply lost your love for someone or lost the will to keep fighting to better that relationship? Sometimes we can spend years fighting for a relationship only to feel that we do not want to have to keep doing so for the rest of our lives. If you feel that a relationship never progresses, it simply bounces back and forth between the same few experiences, or that it has actually gradually worsened over the years then the time might have come to admit your feelings to yourself. If the idea of having a wonderful future relationship with person "X" does not even excite you then you need to decipher what needs to change in order for you to feel excited about the future of that relationship. Either some other aspect of that relationship needs to change that you have yet to address (further goals need setting) *or* you need to distance yourself from that relationship *or* you need to end it altogether. Only you can decide which of the above is true and it's not a decision you can take lightly.

When you look at your relationship vision board, if your chest expands as you take in a breath of self-belief and you feel excited about what you have planned for yourself then you are on the right path. You should maintain this vision board by updating it as and when you can and feel it necessary. Each time you find something that you want to achieve in your relationship add a representation of it to your vision board.

You now know how to write your vision for your ideal relationship in detail, how to visualise it in your mind and how to represent it visually. One last technique to help you propel your relationship from where it is now to where you want it to be is the use of affirmations.

Affirmations can be defined as the act of affirming with a statement or declaration. The statement can be positive or negative but in order to take advantage of the positive power of affirmations one must positively word the affirming statement. It is also important that the affirmations be read and spoken in the present tense as though already achieved. When you state your desires in the present tense you evoke feelings of satisfaction and excitement. When you state your goals in the future tense you induce a state of longing for something unachieved which can create feelings of anxiety and self-doubt. If it has not been achieved you can wonder whether you will achieve it. The purpose of using affirmations is to create the feelings you would experience if you had already successfully achieved your goals. This makes the achievement more believable and as stated in the Bible, "As a man thinketh in his heart, so is he" (Proverbs 23:7). This is a statement that has been made by various philosophers over the years in a number of ways. Earl Nightingale asserted, "We become what we think about." Ralph Waldo Emerson stated, "A man is what he thinks about all day long." It also links with Napoleon Hill's famous quote, "What the mind of man can conceive and believe, it can achieve." The affirmations help you to achieve a state of mind that believes it can achieve, or indeed, that it has already achieved. It is important that you fill your mind with positive thoughts of ability and success, and affirmations are one way in which you can purposely programme your mind in order to better enable the achievement of your goals.

Examples of affirmations that one might employ to better one's relationship might be:

- *My husband and I have a loving, considerate relationship.*
- *My mother gives me the respect I deserve as an adult.*
- *I make friends easily wherever I go.*
- *I am a brilliant parent who knows how to be firm and compassionate.*

Whatever you wish to be and wish to experience you write as though you already are and already experience it.

Now that you know these techniques of visualisation, affirmation and the writing down of your detailed vision of your goals you have some incredibly powerful tools at your disposal. So that you may utilise these techniques to their fullest I shall explain the purpose and power of each a little further.

When you set out to write your goals down in detail you are focusing your mind on your desires. Furthermore, you are creating a vivid, precise picture of what you would like to attract into your life. If you know exactly what you want then you have a much better chance of obtaining it. More importantly still, by creating a detailed account of your goal, how it looks, sounds, smells, feels, and the emotions it produces, you can begin to **believe it possible to obtain** *and* you can get excited about obtaining it. That belief and enthusiasm will propel you to do whatever is necessary to achieve it. Frequently re-reading what you have written is useful as it is with anything you wish to remember at the forefront of your mind. Repetition allows you to build belief on belief and focus on focus. The more you do it, the more belief you will build and the greater your focus will be on achieving it. The mind processes what you put in and so if you purposely program it with good things you can create a life that is fulfilling and rewarding and vice versa. Why else do parents insist that their children keep good company? They know that bad influences will negatively program their children's minds which in turn can create a negative, unrewarding, dissatisfied life experience.

Affirmations are a way to positively program the mind each day very quickly and conveniently. Whilst reading a descriptive account of your desired goals may take some time to complete, the repetition of affirmations can be swiftly completed very easily, at least twice a day. What's more, as you utter your affirmations repeatedly you will soon enough memorise them by heart and thus they will become even more convenient and simple to implement whenever you desire. If you do not manage to say them at any other time at the very least you should repeat them first thing in the morning and last thing at night. By saying them first thing in the morning you set yourself up for the day with a positive mindset. This will then fuel the events of your day positively. You also remind your conscious and subconscious mind of your goals. Consequently you will seek out opportunities and take actions that are conducive to the achievement of those goals. When you say them at night again you focus your mind. This brings relaxation before sleep as you think about your positive, exciting goals. As you are more relaxed at this time of night with fewer distractions you are likely to really focus your mind (what you are thinking) and heart (what you are feeling) on what you are saying. There is also evidence to support the notion that the brain consolidates memories whilst we are sleeping, making them stronger. The sleeping brain even solves problems according to an article by Stickgold and Ellenbogen (2008). Furthermore, though as yet there is limited knowledge about the workings of the sleeping human brain, the fact that we often have dreams related to what we have processed whilst awake (e.g. our thoughts, a film we have watched or a person we have met) would also suggest that the mind is still actively processing when it is asleep. Therefore, to utilise what we do know to our advantage it would be good practice to fill the mind with positive thoughts about the achievement of desired goals rather than of something negative and undesirable. This way the mind will be consolidating your thoughts of goals achieved, as per your affirmations, and may be working on such important matters even when you are sleeping. If the brain is problem solving whilst we are sleeping then by feeding it with instructions of what we desire we may be focusing the brain on solving the challenges we need to overcome in order to achieve our goals.

We have now established that repeating your affirmations morning and night is a good place to start. By repeating each sentence three times before moving on to the next affirmation is also a method advocated by Shad Helmstetter in his book, *What To Say When you Talk To Your Self.* When you try this you will notice a change within your heart and mind each time you repeat the same sentence. There is a shift that takes place from saying it the first time to saying it the third time. The excitement and self-belief and enthusiasm build up. By the end of the third repetition of each affirmation you will be saying it with much more gusto than you began with.

I would also suggest that reading the words aloud will enable you to better commit the statements to your memory. By saying them aloud the brain will remember them through the use of echoic/auditory memory (the memory of what you hear) as well as through iconic/visual memory (the memory of what you see) before you know your affirmations by heart. All of this assists your brain in consolidating such statements into your memory and in your mind so that they become your new set of beliefs about yourself and your life experience.

It is also vital that as you say your affirmations aloud you also feel the emotions within your heart as though you have already achieved the goals. Again, this makes the attainment of your goals feel very real, very believable. As the Institute of HeartMath's research suggests that the heart influences the brain it is especially important that you feel the emotions as real within your heart in order to achieve your goals. It is also a fundamental component of attracting into your life that which you desire if you believe in the law of attraction. Get excited about your goals. They *are* your future if you are willing to see them within your mind, believe them within your heart and take the necessary actions to achieve them.

Visualisation. To assist you in seeing your bright future within your mind, and believing it within your heart, visualisation is a method that has been used by successful athletes to attain success within their field. A striking example of this is cited by LeVan (2009) which demonstrates the power of visualisation and mental practice of something one wishes to attain. LeVan refers to the case of Natan Sharansky, a man accused of spying for the USA who was consequently imprisoned for 9 years in the USSR. During his time in solitary confinement, he mentally played himself in games of chess purely within the confines of his mind. In 1996 Sharansky astoundingly beat the world champion chess player of the time, Garry Kasparov. There are controlled studies that also support the notion that one can practise, improve and attain success simply by utilising the power of visualisation.

Remember your vision board and your detailed written account of your goals? Both techniques assist you in visualising your future as one in which your goals have been achieved. The vision board helps you to envisage what your, in this case, relationship experiences will include and what your relationship will look like. The detailed account of your achieved goals will focus your mind on the more minute details of what the ideal experience will look, sound, feel and smell like. By reviewing your vision board and written account on a regular basis, your mind's vision of your successfully achieved relationship goals becomes clearer and clearer. If you take this information and use it to spend some time relaxing as you close your eyes and visualise your goal then you can let your heart tell your mind that you have achieved the goals already and it is then a case of simply repeating your "previous successes". By visualising and affirming on a daily basis you will be well on your way to achieving your relationship goals.

When you *really* focus on the attainment of a goal you will notice opportunities that allow you to move closer towards them. Only a fool thinks that by solely using affirmations and visualisation the life they dream of will come to fruition. An intelligent man knows that he also has to put in the action required. When you give your mind clear instructions on what you desire two things will happen. Your mind will recognise the opportunities presenting themselves that will move you closer to your goals *and* you will likely want to fulfil your new beliefs that you have programmed into your mind by acting on those opportunities to propel you towards the success that you have predefined. This is why you can still benefit from setting goals that refer to your ideals for someone else's personality or behaviour. By focusing on what you want from them you will notice the signs of it that you might have otherwise missed. By focusing on what you want the other person to become or how you want them to behave means you will identify opportunities for you to help create and nurture such a personality or behaviour in them.

When you purposefully aim to create specific relationships you will positively or negatively affect the outcome of your efforts by the path you choose. If you utilise a path that embraces self-pity and woe and a constant focus on the negatives of what has happened, is happening and could happen then you will create further turmoil within the relationship. If you employ a positive, pro-active approach to achieving your desired relationship and focus on the positives of what has happened, is happening and what can be then you can achieve the most fulfilling, rewarding relationships you can imagine. The choice is yours.

Action Point ----------------------------------
Write down the dates by which you will have achieved the following:

- written your own relationship affirmations,
- constructed your own relationship vision board, and
- written a detailed account of your relationship goals.

Ensure the dates are not too far off in the future but still allow you a realistic time-frame for you to achieve them by.

Ensure you do the above by the dates you have set yourself. The statements you wrote for the exercise in Chapter 3 will assist you.

Once you have created your affirmations, vision board and detailed written account of your ideal relationship it is then time to implement these tools in your day-to-day life. For a continuous period of 90 days do the following:

1. Say your set of affirmations aloud twice daily, morning and night. Utter each individual affirmation three times before you go on to the next one. Consciously listen to what you are saying and consciously feel how you will feel once you have achieved them.
2. When you are relaxed, and there are no distractions, look at your vision board at least twice a week for at least 90 seconds. As you look at the images get excited about the fact that this is what you are going to experience in your relationship(s).
3. Twice a week when you are relaxed and there are no distractions, close your eyes and either sit back or lie down. For 90 seconds visualise your relationship experiences as you would ideally like them to be as though you have already attained them. Imagine as vividly as you can and let the corresponding emotions run through your mind and body as you do.
4. Read your detailed account of your ideal relationship(s) once a month.

If you do the above you will absolutely notice a positive change in the relationship(s) that you wish to improve. It is very possible that you will begin to notice positive changes within 30 days but by following this regime for 90 days you will better propel your relationships from where they are now to where you want them to be.

The number of positive changes that arise as a result of your 90 day commitment will also be far greater than if you follow this regime for 30 days. Follow it to the letter and not only will you reap the rewards for this part of your life but you will then believe in the power of implementing such techniques and then successfully apply them to other aspects of your life.

The question is: are you willing to spend just a few minutes each day to help turn your flailing relationship(s) around?

Chapter 19

Don't Get Washed Away

"The older I get the more I try not to waste my time on negative energy."

- Christine Baranski

In the previous chapter we looked at how what we do, say, think and feel impacts on our lives at a much deeper level than many realise. What you attract into your life and what you repel from your life all begins with the thinking process. When you behave in a certain way it is because of the thoughts you have had which you have evaluated in a particular way that have subsequently led to your resulting behaviours (as first explored in Chapter 4). These results that you experience inform your future thoughts and you control all of these thoughts in your mind.

If you think of your mind as the starting point from which all life experiences develop you understand the significance of controlling what you feed your brain. You are aware that you must control your thoughts, even to the point of manipulating what you selectively allow into your mind so that you can manufacture your own life experiences, including your relationship experiences. No matter how wonderful a gatekeeper you are, you will sometimes allow some counter-productive negatives to slip through. The question is: what do you let into your mind without even thinking about it?

The people around you emit their own agendas. These often consist of problems and negativities. It is not that the people in your life necessarily want to burden you so much as they want to unburden themselves. What they often don't realise is that what they offload may begin to affect you negatively. By learning how to separate your own thoughts and beliefs from those of others you can still be their emotional support without becoming a victim of their thoughts.

When you are dealing with the stories of others remember that you do not have the whole story. You must not blindly adopt the beliefs of others as you do not know the reasons they have come to the point in their lives where they hold such beliefs. Tell yourself, "I control my thoughts and beliefs. I decide what I should believe in."

Now if you are being bombarded with the thoughts and beliefs of those you do not feel the need to provide support to then simply try to distance yourself from them. Have you noticed how moaning work colleagues or neighbours can reduce your own morale when they are bombarding your mind with negative thoughts and beliefs they hold? If you are in a target driven career you need to limit such experiences with negative colleagues or they will affect your productivity, results and income. Sometimes it can be easier to distance yourself from these people, limiting the time you spend around them.

Some people are simply going through a tough time in their lives, at work or personally, and they can enter into a negative bubble, if you like. Such people need guidance and help out of the negative bubble and if they are important to you, you can teach them what you have learnt in this book. On the other hand, if they are simply an associate rather than a friend and you struggle to pull them out of their bubble of negativity then dissociate yourself from them once you find you are becoming negatively affected by their negativity. You will know if they negatively affect you by the way you feel when you bump into them or when you walk away from them.

If you ever catch yourself thinking something that you know has been uttered by the negative person and you know that you did not used to think this way and/or you do not really believe this then that is a clear sign that they are affecting your thoughts negatively. If you allow this to happen you will then base your emotions on these negatively altered thoughts which will lead to negative behaviours and negative results. I'm not suggesting that you become selfish or cold hearted by any means. What I am suggesting is that you step away from the negative people in your life if you do not have, nor wish to have, a meaningful relationship with them.

What becomes increasingly difficult is when you have people in your life that are negatively affecting your life over and over and over again and yet they *are* someone you have a meaningful relationship with. If you love someone but they are hurting you and your life it can be difficult to manage.

Some people thrive off drama and stress and some people simply adore a constant element of drama and stress in their lives. This may sound ridiculous but you may actually know somebody like this.

A research study conducted by Joseph et al. (2009) looked at the brain functions of people who sought out adrenaline related activities ("high thrill seekers"), such as sky diving, and those that did not ("low thrill seekers"). They discovered that the high thrill seekers found adrenaline inducing events arousing in the same part of the brain that a drug addict is aroused, the insula. On the other hand, low thrill seekers were not aroused in the insula part of the brain during such adrenaline inducing activities. Furthermore, during adrenaline inducing events the high thrill seekers' brains did not activate the emotion controlling parts of the brain in the frontal cortex whilst the low thrill seekers' brains did. The researchers concluded that this is why, for example, low thrill seekers will fear prospective dangers of adrenaline inducing events whilst high thrill seekers will not. Therefore, those who thrive off stress, drama and chaos perhaps seek this behaviour as a way of getting an adrenaline fix in the same way that a drug addict seeks to satisfy their addiction with a drug fix.

Can you think of anyone you know who seems to go from one drama to the next to the next? When you think about what has happened in their life can you see the part that they themselves have played in creating the upheavals? Whatever your set of beliefs it is unlikely that you would consider a person who spends decades of their life bouncing from one drama to the next as innocent and unlucky. We create the life we live. Sure sometimes bad things happen to all of us. Some will say this is karma and so we personally created it. Some will say we were just unlucky. Some will say it was meant to be and there is a purpose for it. Whatever your belief system you would not believe someone was so doomed that they spent their life going from one drama to the next constantly for ten, twenty, thirty years. It doesn't happen, at least, not without that person's own input. The victim in these scenarios is often the perpetrator.

If you spend a considerable amount of time around such perpetrators you will inevitably become affected. People who create negativity in their life will create negativity in your life if you spend a considerable amount of time with them. Fact! The scary thing is that we don't always realise this until the affect has taken place. These relationships in your life may be the sort of relationships you cannot easily sever or do not wish to eliminate altogether. They may be a parent, child, sibling or partner, for example. When these relationships negatively affect you they have a knock-on effect on your other relationships and the other aspects of your life. Such experiences do not operate in isolation. At the very least they affect our morale, our happiness, our stress levels and our feeling of life satisfaction. They can even affect our ethics and our personality, changing them for the worse. As how we think, feel and behave changes, our relationships can suffer negative consequences.

If you are struggling with any of your relationships you need to be aware of what external influences are internally changing the way you are now responding to your life and the relationships within it. Have you become more aggressive in your manner than you used to be and is this now affecting those close to you? Are you becoming more of a worrier and dragging this into your relationships and thus dragging the fun out of them? Have you become unhappy and lost the energy to do the things that keep that spark alive in your relationships? The way in which the contrived drama and negativity of others around you washes through your life can be so unnoticeable at first that you may not realise what has happened until the drops of negative energy have built up to bucket loads and you suddenly find yourself being washed downstream with them. Get out of the way before you drown your own relationships in someone else's need for an adrenaline rush.

Now of course that is easier said than done, right? Well, sometimes, yes. If you live in the same house it is difficult to separate yourself from the drama. One thing you can do in such circumstances is immerse yourself in your own life, thus allowing less time for the negativity to touch your life. Secondly, when you do come into contact with these chaotic personalities, be it because you live with them or not, there are ways you can limit the effects that their latest self-made drama has on your life.

To begin with, do not rise to it. Do not get involved with the drama. Separate yourself from the negativity. Even if the drama personally involves you, let it be known that you are keeping your distance. The best way to do this is to stay silent and remain non-confrontational. This power of staying silent is a great way of communicating to the other person and anyone else that may have been dragged into the drama, that you do not give your permission to be pulled into the commotion. The situation will usually defuse as the days and weeks go by. Sometimes unsuspecting good-doers will help this person satisfy their craving for drama by getting involved and giving them the attention they would like. Others will be affected by the drama by failing to stand back when the bonfire is lit and as a result satisfy the person's need for drama. Other times the situation will defuse as a result of the flames not being fanned. When drama-seekers receive little or no response they will usually move on and the fire will go out. If it is necessary to defend yourself then it is better to do so after some time has lapsed after you have remained away from the drama initially and allowed the drama-seeker time to calm down. Your initial silence will not only let the person know that you do not wish to entertain their latest need for drama, you also assert your own self-worth and your own sense of power. Furthermore, you inadvertently let them know that their manufactured drama is of a much lower importance than any positive experiences that you share. This is reminiscent of what I discussed earlier, whereby you practise not reinforcing bad behaviour.

When you spend your life around the instigators of artificial drama you will invite at least some of the negative by-products into your own life. Remember that like attracts like.

Case Study ----------------------------------
"Jim" worked in an environment where he was expected to manage his department in a way that his superior saw fit. His boss, "Ryan", was a man who fuelled his own sense of importance through the drama and stress he himself created as well as by denigrating his workforce.

As the number of dramas added up so did the tension amongst the staff. Jim began to find himself cringing at Ryan's management style and feeling embarrassed to have to uphold it as a middle manager. Jim also began dreading all meetings with Ryan as they would invariably consist of drama, stress and aggravation.

Jim found that Ryan's negative, stressful outward behaviour was beginning to affect how he himself was now managing the staff. He found himself getting lost in the chaos. He wanted to manage the staff and the day-to-day running of the business in an intelligent, uplifting, pro-active, smooth operation but felt himself being yanked towards the stress, drama and negativity on a daily basis.

The knock-on effect was clearly taking place, transferred from the drama-loving boss to him and on towards the staff.

Jim began to resent working there. The constant belittling that Ryan inflicted on others for his own personal satisfaction and tension release led Jim to begin to doubt himself and his abilities even though deep down he knew he was very capable. Jim would feel ashamed of himself for being rude to others because of the work environment that he was in that seemed to expect such behaviour of him. He began to feel glum at the weekends which meant that he didn't want to go anywhere. He didn't feel good about himself and he didn't feel good about the place he spent so much of his time.

As the months went by and Jim's dissatisfaction and stress intensified he started to offload anecdotes of work experiences by sharing them with his girlfriend. Although he retained much of his heartache and worry to himself, Jim's girlfriend still began to feel fed up with the stories, and Jim understood why. After all, they were essentially the same story repeated with only slight variations. The crux of the stories was that the boss was insufferable and the workforce was unhappy and unmotivated. The result was a discontent boyfriend at home who was upset and angry. This affected the boyfriend-girlfriend relationship too as the stress and unhappiness was being brought into their home life. Ryan's self-engineered dramas and stresses had dragged Jim underneath the currents at work, were now beginning to wash over Jim's relationship with his partner and were meandering towards his relationships with his parents and siblings. Jim's parents and siblings too were feeling the brunt of Ryan's dramas as they experienced the unhappiness of their close family member.

Fortunately, Jim began to notice that he was drowning in a world he did not want to be a part of any longer. He realised the disparity between his personality, morals, and ideas about relationships and desirable life experiences, and those of his boss. The negative impact of the association with a person such as Ryan had taken effect on his own life quite profoundly but he eventually recognised this and decided to remove himself from the experience. Jim changed jobs and thus removed the unnecessary, fabricated drama and stress. Jim went on to have an enjoyable, fulfilling career and home-life whilst Ryan apparently went on to create more drama.

Perhaps an evaluation of your own life will reveal that you do not have anyone creating unnecessary drama on a frequent basis. However, if you do, are you a Ryan or are you a Jim? In other words, do you create these experiences or do you only suffer as a result of someone else creating them?

Action Point
Write down the names of anyone you think may be creating unnecessary drama in your life that is having a negative knock-on effect on the relationship(s) you want to improve.

Write down examples of:

- when the drama-seeker has done this,
- how it affected how you *feel* about yourself and others,

- how it affected how you have *behave* towards yourself and others,
- how it has negatively impacted the relationship(s) that you are looking to repair.

Next, write down a discussion of how you can minimise or eliminate the negativity, stress and drama that the drama-seeker is inflicting on your life and on your relationships.

Finally, follow your plan to eliminate unnecessary drama from your life lest you lose a relationship to it.

Chapter 20

For Best Results Bake Until Risen

"Whenever you're in conflict with someone, there is one factor that can make the difference between damaging your relationship and deepening it. That factor is attitude."

- William James

In life we must treat others as we would like to be treated. Of course, dare I say it again, like attracts like and people will respond in likeness to how you respond to them. Whilst there are a number of important factors that determine healthy personal relationship experiences, the key ingredients are:

- Love
- Trust
- Respect
- Communication
- Friendship
- Commitment

Love. Without love for one another you will not battle your way through the adversities that your relationship brings. If we love someone we will always try to keep the relationship moving forward successfully. We work through the bumps in the relationship's road. We look for solutions. When we fall out of love we stop trying to make the relationship work. This is why family relationships are much more difficult to break because there tends be a deep-seated love that anchors both parties, no matter how difficult the relationship can sometimes become.

Without love for yourself you will not be able to love others and they will struggle to love you. It is the love between human beings that makes our existence feel worthwhile. It is the love transferred from parent to child that ensures the child feels secure. It is the love transferred from child to parent that ensures that the aging parent is looked after, particularly in Eastern cultures. It is the love between friends that keeps the person sane and secure when the going gets tough.

Trust. Complete trust may sometimes be missing but without any trust whatsoever there would be no relationship to speak of. Complete trust provides serenity, reassurance and security within the relationship. If the trust is broken it must be rebuilt and it is not always possible depending on the people involved. Some find it impossible to trust someone again once their trust has been broken. Others can be more understanding and forgiving.

Trust allows you to spend time away from a person without fear of being betrayed. Trust allows you to live independently of those you love without the need to keep an eye on them or feel that you and your behaviour is under a microscope.

Trust comes from a capacity to be honest. The transparency of who you are at your core builds trust. Your ability to keep your word and tell the truth in day to day life shows those you have meaningful relationships with that you are trustworthy. You do not have to perform any amazing feats to prove your integrity. It's the small things that speak volumes to those watching. Sincerity in the mind translates in what you are saying and doing to others. If you fake sincerity it usually shows in the eyes. You cannot fabricate it for long. You are either sincere or you are not.

If you are insincere you need to realise that you cannot trick people for long, if at all. The word facade may serve as a reminder of the futility of this approach to relationships. An acronym I have created sums it up pretty well:

Fools **A**re **C**aught **A**s **D**eceit **E**merges.

To think that you can insincerely convince people of your sincerity is foolish.

Respect must be earned and retained. It must also be awarded to the other people you have relationships with. They too must earn and retain your respect. If either party is not respected at all, your relationship will meet an inevitable end. If the level of respect for either person in a relationship is low the feeling of relationship satisfaction will be low as well. A lack of respect eats away at the victim's self-worth. When a person feels lacking in worth he can become depressed, insecure, angry, bitter and self-pitying which in turn will have a negative impact on the relationship.

When one person has created a lack of trust or respect with their actions, they need to earn it back by behaving in a way that invites the now missing ingredient. Both parties need to definitively explore what is expected and essential in order for the trust or respect to be regained. The insightful instructions must then be acted upon. If after a reasonable amount of time *and* effort the person in question has not managed to earn back the trust and/or respect then both parties will need to assess whether the relationship is salvageable.

Communication is the key that will unlock the answers to problems, resolve misunderstandings, convey love and passion, remove insecurities and instil friendship, to name a few. Without communication there is no relationship. That communication can be verbal or non-verbal. Without it you do not build relationships, you cannot consolidate relationships and you certainly cannot repair relationships. If there is a breakdown in communication there will be a breakdown in your relationship.

If someone stops communicating with you not only should the alarm bells ring in your mind but you should also realise that this is their way of telling you something – perhaps that they just don't care about their relationship with you. They don't have to say they don't care if they are showing you they don't care. Similarly, if you have stopped communicating with someone who was important in your life then you have stopped fighting for that relationship.

If you stand by your decision to not communicate and intend to keep it this way then you may as well pack your (mental) bags and go. This despondency is a clear sign that you have subconsciously given up on the relationship, albeit temporarily. At this point it is not necessarily the end. You may have simply shut down your attempts to fight for your relationships without progressing to the point of termination. Different people will do this for different reasons. It may be that you have tried communicating to make things work but you have failed and now feel dejected. It may be that you feel stumped, confused almost, and need time to process what is happening. This is not necessarily a bad thing. Time out can give you the space and time you might need to process what is happening in your troubled relationship. This time out can bring clarity. Clarity about what the relationship means to you. Clarity about where the relationship is headed if its course remains unchanged. Clarity about where the relationship experience is going wrong and what is creating the problems. Clarity about your next move, in other words, what you will now do in order to get the relationship back on track.

Friendship is the foundation on which the best relationships grow. When a sense of friendship bonds you and your partner, parent, sibling, child or indeed friend, there is a meeting of minds that connects you to a powerful feeling. This feeling consists of empathy, energy, tranquillity and joy. This meeting of minds is good for the soul and important for longevity. Dayton (2010) references a study conducted between two universities that evaluated data spanning over three decades. Co-author of the study, Timothy Smith, stated that their findings indicate that people who are better connected socially will live an average of 3.7 years longer than people with a less-connected social life. Therefore, healthy relationships are a contributing factor to long life.

It is worth remembering that a sense of friendship always bonds people further than the relationship by blood or marriage or romantic interest does on its own. When you base your relationships on friendship you are saying, "You mean more to me than merely the DNA that ties us together" or "You mean more to me than merely the romantic feelings we have for one another."

Commitment does not solely stem from swearing an oath or taking vows. It is the commitment in your heart and mind to do whatever is necessary (within reason) to maintain and nurture a relationship you have with someone. If either party lacks commitment your relationship will perish at the hurdles. It's the commitment that gives you staying power and fighting power in the face of adversities. It's the commitment that removes the risk of complacency within the relationship. It's the commitment that makes you constantly strive to better your relationships.

It is not enough to assume that all will work out. Some people believe that, for example, just because there is a huge amount of love between them and their spouse and just because they believe they will absolutely spend the rest of their lives together that they needn't commit to making the experience the best it can be. There is a difference between spending the rest of your lives together extremely happily and spending it having a mediocre experience. Your level of commitment to improve, to repair, to love and to care is in direct proportion with the rewards you reap in your relationships.

When dealing with fellow human beings it is necessary to remember that one size does not fit all. What I mean by that is that different people have different ideas of love, trust, respect, communication, friendship and commitment. Sometimes when you have been in a relationship with someone for some time you can begin to notice that perhaps they don't quite share the same ideas as you about the ingredients that go into a successful relationship. This can be due to a change in personality. People can change, for better or worse, through the course of their lifetime.

Therefore, you may know someone for a long time that has changed in their way of being. This can bring an upheaval of emotions if the change is perceived as for the worse, especially if it is long after the beginning of your relationship.

A change in someone's personality may come about as a result of life experiences they have had. Such experiences may have changed the way they now perceive the world around them. A consequence might be a lack of any one of the key ingredients for a healthy relationship. Only you can decide if you are willing and believe it possible to work through the imbalance to get your relationship back on track and back into a state of equilibrium. You might decide that you are willing to maintain a relationship with that person but perhaps to a lesser degree than you have previously. The term keeping someone at arm's length might be symbolic of how you wish to move forward.

If, however, you believe that you are willing to forgo the joys of being in a healthy balanced relationship without even an attempt to work at recreating the balance, then something is wrong. If this rings true for you then why is it that you are you selling yourself short? Do you deserve the happiness of a mutually loving, trusting, respectful, communicative, friendly, committed relationship? Of course you do. Whether that be with your family, friends or partner, anything less is unfair on you. Don't you tell yourself that it is okay. You must not hastily settle for second best. Sure some people would rather be in a somewhat less than fully satisfying relationship than be alone and that is fair enough. Each person carries his own standards for his life experiences but I am simply asking that you give improvement a concerted effort first.

Strive to have the best relationships that you can in life because the value they will add to your life experience and lifetime successes is immense. Fantastic relationships empower us to feel that we can take on any challenges in life. They give us the courage to succeed and the self-belief that we can achieve greatness.

Chapter 21
Feel Your Way

"All great men are gifted with intuition. They know without reasoning or analysis, what they need to know."

- Alexis Carrel

Sometimes you get an eerie feeling when you walk into an unknown establishment and you do not know why, you just know you do not like the feeling you are experiencing. Other times you feel that you do not want to hire an employee or strike up an instant friendship with someone because something inside you tells you there may be trouble up ahead.

You might recall a situation when you did something, went somewhere, feeling a little uneasy. You ignored the feeling and still proceeded to go. The experience turned out to be an undesirable one and you wished you hadn't gone. You probably said to yourself, "I *knew* I shouldn't have gone." Nevertheless, you still had. In the modern day, some would argue that you should have followed your gut instinct or trusted your intuition but what do they actually mean? What is it that you should have followed or trusted and how can this immensely help you and your relationships?

The words instinct and intuition tend to be used interchangeably in modern society and whilst some will define the word intuition as being more relevant to generalities whilst instinct is more applicable to survival, we shall not get bogged down with that right now. As a modern day reader I think you will understand why I too will use the terms interchangeably here. After all, it is generally understood what the author is saying when one reads the word instinct or intuition in the context within which it is written. However, before I do I will offer you a brief definition of each, as per the *Cambridge Dictionaries Online*.

Instinct is defined as "the way people or animals naturally react or behave, without having to think or learn about it".

Intuition is defined as "(knowledge from) an ability to understand or know something immediately without needing to think about it, learn it or discover it by using reason".

A study conducted by Voss and Paller (2009) supports the notion that intuition does exist and it is the process of tapping into memories that are embedded within our brains at a more subconscious level rather than at the conscious level. Participants in the study were given images to memorise. Half of the images were memorised whilst being distracted whilst the other half were memorised by paying full attention. When the participants were later tested for their memory of these images the researchers discovered that there was significantly greater accuracy for recalling the images that had been memorised during distractions than the images memorised with full attention. Even when utilising guesswork the guesses were more accurate for the images memorised during distractions than those memorised without distractions. The results indicate that the brain accesses information that is not necessarily stored at a conscious level, hence the success of using what people refer to as a gut feeling. We can make decisions based on what we think is right although conscious reasoning may not be taking place. With the results of new research by the Institute of HeartMath demonstrating how intelligent the heart is at sending signals to the entire body and beyond, plus its ability to store its own memories, perhaps the heart too is responsible for these gut feelings, perhaps more so than the brain itself.

Clearly a great deal more research is yet to be done to enable a much deeper understanding of how we use intuition, what is involved and how accurate it is. It is worth noting, however, that many successful entrepreneurs claim that they access their gut instinct for major decisions in business.

At some point in our lives we have probably all been asked by someone, "What does your gut feeling tell you to do?" or "What does your gut instinct say?", or something to that effect. Can you remember a time when someone has asked you to tap into this part of your inner self? Did you find that sometimes the answer to a question just feels so very obvious all of a sudden and other times you are still unsure?

To help you understand how to tap into your gut intuition so that you can use it in your relationships, career, social situations and so on, I'll take you through a series of scenarios.

When some people struggle to decide between two options, unable to access their gut feeling someone might offer to choose an option for them. This thought of someone else taking control of the decision making process can sometimes force the person into recognising which option they would like to go for before *or* after the other party has made the choice on their behalf. Allow me to demonstrate this with a generic example.

Example -
Harry and Joe are best friends and housemates. It is midday on a Saturday and they sit discussing their options for the day. It's the weekend and after a week at work, as always, they would like to make the most of the afternoon. Joe has plans with his family whilst Harry is still unsure as to what to do. As Harry struggles to decide how to spend his Saturday he thinks of three possible options that he cannot choose between. He could stay at home relaxing in front of the TV with snacks and drinks and simply let his body recuperate as he feels tired. On the other hand he could go play some crazy golf with a friend and perhaps grab a drink after. A third option in his mind is going for a late lunch with a friend.

Harry struggles to decide on one course of action as the tug of war in his mind is pulling him between the desire to rest and the desire to make the most of his free time. Weekends are soon over and he is aware that time is so precious as once it is lost it cannot be regained. He also wants to ensure that he does not grow old and look back at his life with regret of not having experienced the pleasures of life and having wasted his life away in front of a TV set. After wasting an hour of his morning feeling indecisive and bouncing ideas back and forth in his mind he enlists Joe's help in coming to a decision.

Harry explains that he is in a quandary and asks Joe to decide for him. Joe says, "Well, why don't you go out for lunch with Mike? You keep saying you need to get together with him because it's been a while."

"Hmmm. Could do. Not sure I can be bothered seeing Mike today though."

"What about going to play crazy golf with Jeremy? He'll be up for that."

"Yeah, I don't know if I can be bothered walking around."

"Why don't you just relax at home then?"

"I just don't want to get to Monday morning and think that I didn't achieve anything or do anything worthwhile."

"Go out then. Go and play some crazy golf, get a drink after, enjoy your weekend. You'll have a laugh. I think you should definitely go out with Jeremy."

Harry finally reached a decision. "I think I will stay at home."

Harry found himself better able to recognise what he wanted to do as a result of being pushed towards an option that did not really match his true inner desires. He had been having a tug of war between what he thought he wanted to do and what he really wanted to do. He was now able to recognise what he wanted to do by Joe pushing him away from his true desire. The threat of doing something that he did not want to do and the threat of not being able to do that which he truly desired guided Harry towards his true desire by unearthing it to make it accessible to his conscious mind. This act of shutting off the other option can in itself sometimes lead to an easier decision making process.

Now let's look at the same example with a slightly different ending.

Example ------------------------------------

Harry explains that he is in a quandary and asks Joe to decide for him. Joe says, "Well, why don't you go out for lunch with Mike? You keep saying you need to get together with him because it's been a while."

"Hmmm. Could do. Not sure I can be bothered seeing Mike today though."

"What about going to play crazy golf with Jeremy? He'll be up for that."

"Yeah, I don't know if I can be bothered walking around."

"Why don't you just relax at home then?"

"I just don't want to get to Monday morning and think that I didn't achieve anything or do anything worthwhile."

"I don't know what to suggest. You sound like you can't be bothered to go out though."

"Yeah, I think you're right. I am feeling tired and lazy. I've been working hard recently. Maybe I should just relax and have some time out. Cheers Joe."

"For what?" asks Joe.

"For helping me decide."

"I didn't do anything. You decided for yourself."

Joe is quite right, Harry did decide for himself but by acting as a sounding board Joe helped Harry to hear himself - his inner self.

Harry wanted to stay at home all along. He needed to. His body was tired and his mind was tired. The only reason Harry was feeling torn between the options was that he was feeling guilty for not honouring his intention to make the most out of life. He was fearful of any potential regret on Monday morning and trying to prevent it. He was focused on so many other factors that he forgot to "listen to his heart". One might say that when his heart was saying to rest, his mind was saying he should make the most of his leisure time.

Joe astutely noticed that Joe had given reasons, or made excuses, for not going for lunch with Mike or playing crazy golf with Jeremy. Remember that Harry gave Joe notice of the three possible options that he was considering. If Harry really wanted to go out for lunch but simply didn't want to go out with Mike he could have altered Joe's suggestion of going with Mike to going for lunch with someone else instead. Had he wanted to go out with Jeremy but did not want to play crazy golf he could have decided on an alternative activity. Had he wanted to do something other than lunch or crazy golf or had he wanted to spend the day with someone else altogether he also could have suggested that too. The fact that he had neglected to entertain alternative options within his mind demonstrated his lack of desire for going out.

When you want something you search for ways to obtain it, be it an experience or an object or someone's affection. By recognising your own willing or lack thereof you can understand your inner desires. As Joe reflected back to Harry his perception of what Harry appeared to be conveying, Harry was able to hear his own inner desires.

Now let's look at this example slightly differently again.

Example -
Harry explains that he is in a quandary and asks Joe to decide for him. Joe says, "Well, why don't you go out for lunch with Mike? You keep saying you need to get together with him because it's been a while."

"Hmmm. Could do. Not sure I can be bothered seeing Mike today though."

"What about going to play crazy golf with Jeremy? He'll be up for that."

"Yeah, I don't know if I can be bothered walking around. Thinking about it I'm actually just so tired that I haven't the energy to make conversation with people let alone walk around or even go out for food. Hmmm, I just need some rest. Home, television and snacks it is!"

- -

Sometimes you just need to work through your feelings. The process of discussing your options over with someone else can help. Even if you are alone and you have no one to talk to, you can talk aloud to yourself. Ask yourself questions out loud such as the example, "Do I really want to go out with Mike for lunch?" Answer your questions aloud also. Bounce the questions back and forth, forcing yourself to unearth your true inner desires. Think of an archaeologist who delicately brushes the soil away to reveal the precious artefact underneath. By steadily brushing away the upper layers of your thoughts and feelings you too can unearth your precious true desires and feelings.

A fourth example, the third one with a variation of the first, is as follows.

Example -
Harry and Joe are best friends and housemates. It is midday on a Saturday and they sit discussing their options for the day. It's the weekend and after a week at work, as always, they would like to make the most of the afternoon. Joe has plans with his family whilst Harry is still unsure as to what to do.

Harry sits and ponders how to spend his Saturday. He thinks of three possible options that he initially finds appealing. He could stay at home relaxing in front of the TV with snacks and drinks and simply let his body recuperate as he feels tired. On the other hand he could go play some crazy golf with a friend and perhaps grab a drink after. A third option in his mind is going for a late lunch with a friend.

The weekend is soon over and he is aware that time is so precious as once it is lost it cannot be regained. He also wants to ensure that he does not grow old and look back at his life with regret of not having experienced the pleasures of life and having wasted his life away in front of a TV set.

As he sits there thinking Harry listens to the signals of his thoughts and emotions that arise as he entertains each idea of how to spend the day. In other words he listens to the signals of his mind *and* body. He asks himself what feels like the right option and is rapidly able to identify how each of the three options feels. If neither felt right he would search for an alternative but as it happens one of the options feels right and two do not. He chooses the one that feels right and that is to stay at home and relax and recuperate. At the end of the weekend Harry feels so incredibly energised that he smiles to himself. Harry turns to Joe on that Sunday evening and says, "I feel so much better. I clearly needed a good rest this weekend. I'm so glad I didn't go out or do anything strenuous. I feel full of energy and excitement about the week ahead now!"

Harry was very quickly able to identify his gut feelings and subsequently make what, in hindsight, was evidently a great decision. It was likely the *best* decision too but without knowing the outcome of the other experiences in this scenario (as they were not tested) one cannot categorically state that this was the case.

What Harry was able to do in that final example is something you too can learn to do. Whilst some people are naturally better at paying attention to their gut feeling and believe in the importance of doing so, others can obtain and develop the skills and adopt the same attitude. The goal is that you become aware of the importance of utilising this aspect of human reasoning, access it without fail as and when required, and thus live the life you truly desire and achieve all the successes that you are capable of achieving.

When you are able to almost instantly, if not instantly, locate your gut feeling about something, someone or somewhere, that is when you can say that you are able to follow your gut instinct, gut feeling or intuition. This fast thinking-and-feeling ability is what enables you to rely inwards when you need to make decisions. This is especially helpful when you need to make a decision fast based on the information you have. This is also especially useful if you cannot solicit the help of another person nor obtain any further information to help you make a decision.

In the example given, Harry used his gut feeling to decide something relatively small - how to spend his day off.

Using intuition when you are evaluating your next move in the game of life works in just the same way. The difference is that for major life decisions the sole use of intuition carries a much bigger responsibility as you are hedging your bets on a feeling rather than (conscious) facts. Likewise, it can be the provider of much bigger rewards too. For this reason it is well worth adopting into your own decision making process. The ease with which you can flow through life by following your gut feeling is incredible. It brings real peace of mind.

Now let's explore the "how-to" of using physical sensations to identify your gut instinct. When you find yourself in a predicament and divided between your options your gut feeling will tell you which *feels* better. Next time you find yourself in such a situation think of each option as though you are choosing that option. When you mentally choose that option you need to acknowledge the feelings you get in various parts of your body. The reason for this is that your body does respond physically and physiologically to the emotions that you are feeling. It can, therefore, be easier to notice your body's physical response to an emotion than the emotion itself.

In particular you should pay attention to the feeling in the left-hand side of your chest (around your heart), the feeling in your throat, the feeling in your back and the feeling in your scalp. You may notice a tight feeling in your chest around the heart, a lump in your throat, stiffened back muscles or a tightening of the scalp. These sensations, or a lack of, can provide clear signs that you feel negatively or positively about a particular option you are considering.

There are in fact a number of physical symptoms that can occur when you are considering your possible options during a decision making process. Those that arise in *your* body are specific to you. Learn to look out for them and you will soon realise which are *your* tell-tale signs that something does not *feel* good or right. When looking out for good-feeling tell-tale signs that the option you are considering is the right one, you may experience a feeling of euphoria. On the other hand you may find that the parts of your body that feel tense when something does not feel right, feel relaxed when you are considering options that do feel good and right.

There may be other signs that you may notice in places such as your hands, feet, arms, legs, stomach, breathing, etc. The list of possibilities is quite extensive.

Think about how you may have interpreted someone else's reaction to something in the past. For example, you may have noticed that someone was nervous, not by what they said but by the constant fidgeting of their hands or feet. When someone you know has been feeling stressed out or worried you may have noticed them biting their lips and read this as a sign of their anxiety even though they had not verbally alerted you to the fact that they were feeling this way. These actions can occur as a result of inner thoughts becoming automatically translated into a physical response. You do not control this unless you consciously make a concerted effort to. Therefore, you can use these non-verbal cues to assist in your decision making process about which of your options is the correct one to opt for.

So you see, by evaluating your physical and emotional response to something you can assess which one of several options appears to be the right one. What is your internal dialogue saying? What is it not saying? What are your body's sensations suggesting? How nervous and anxious do you feel about a particular option? How excited, comfortable, relaxed and optimistic do you feel about a given option? These are the questions to ask yourself when you wish to implement your intuition.

One other pattern you will notice over time as you pay attention to this process is that the *very first* instinctive thought in your mind is often the right one, *even when* that first answer only flashes in your mind for a fleeting moment. If you recall, studies by Voss and Paller and the Institute of HeartMath were cited earlier in the chapter. Voss and Paller's research suggested that the brain scans *all* stored information when trying to recall a memory; the Institute of HeartMath's research suggested that the heart stores its own memories and influences the organs of the human body. Therefore, at these early stages of empirical research we can consider this instinctive first thought as the possible result of a rapid scan of all files stored in memory by the sophisticated human heart and brain. By adopting the belief that this is wholly possible, the inclination to treat this instinctive first thought as accidental can be replaced with an appreciation of how clever your heart and brain actually are and how they can purposefully assist you in making correct decisions in life.

As time goes by, if you practise the use of intuition you will find that it becomes more finely tuned. As such the concerted effort you apply when utilising it will become reduced as the process will become more natural to you. Not only will the use of your gut feeling become more natural to you but you will also begin to elicit your answers extremely speedily if not instantaneously.

Armed with this knowledge you must now apply it to the troubled relationship in your life that you are seeking to remedy.

First of all you need to harness the power of resolve to see you through the arduous task of relationship repair. Using your gut feeling, you must evaluate the option of maintaining a relationship with person "X" in your life and the option of not maintaining a relationship with person "X" in your life. If you decide that you *do* want to maintain a life-long relationship with this person then you need to fight for this relationship all the way through the hurdles. You will then know that, no matter how hard it becomes and how little you feel the relationship is moving forward positively, there is no giving up. This mentality will ensure you keep searching for solutions whenever you come up against problems. You might view this in similar terms to the theory of the fight-or-flight response to danger. You will either flee from the relationship or you will fight for its success.

Some of you will be wondering whether you want to maintain a relationship with someone, perhaps a romantic partner, or end the relationship and look for a better one. This is why you must decide deep within whether you are fighting for it or fleeing from it. You may have an extremely difficult relationship with someone and decide that you don't want to flee from it altogether but that you need distance from it. Again, your gut feeling will tell you how to proceed. The decision may be that you will maintain the relationship but at arm's length. In other words, you do not want to lose the person from your life altogether but you want to keep the interaction to a minimum. However, chances are that you are reading this book because you wholeheartedly want to fight for a relationship and significantly improve it.

Secondly, think about what it is that is going wrong in the relationship that you are looking to remedy. Which of the key ingredients of the relationship are missing: love, trust, respect, communication, friendship or commitment? Who is responsible for the lacking ingredients, you, them or both of you? What does your gut feeling tell you. This is not a blame game nor should you absolve the other of their responsibility in the part they have played in the downfall of the relationship. When you know which ingredient or ingredients are missing and who is responsible for neglecting to bring them into the relationship, you can then consider the courses of action you can potentially take as per the previous discussion of relationship remedies within this book.

Each course of action you intend to take will give rise to gut feelings about the actions themselves and whether or not they will produce the desired effects within your relationship with person "X". Each time you relate to one another you will have a gut feeling about whether or not it felt positive or negative, like growth or decline. You can then monitor this gut feeling feedback to gage how you intend to move forward. As you become adept at following your intuition you will stop beating yourself up over mistakes and bad choices made as there will be significantly fewer of them.

When you are able to access your gut feeling you will feel better about yourself and improve your relationship with yourself. The better your relationship with yourself the better your relationships with others will be.

When it comes to your relationships in life, those you have now and those you will have in the future, you will always find that the answers lie deep within about how you feel about the other person, their behaviour, their attitude, how much involvement you want with them, how to broach your relationship problems with them and how to maintain a fantastic relationship with them. You can make the *right choices* by *feeling* your way towards them. When it comes to your relationships the answers lie deep within. Tap into them. Listen to them. Have the guts to follow them.

Appendix

SMART Goals are goals that are clearly defined, quantifiable goals with a date set for achieving them by.

SMART is an acronym for:

Specific **M**easurable **A**ttainable **R**elevant **T**ime-bound

Examples:

I will have written my relationship affirmations by 8pm on 27/05/12

Each Saturday at 6pm my husband and I will spend at least three hours doing a fun, interactive activity together that we both enjoy.

It is advisable to write all of your goals down using this technique, for all aspects of your life.

References

Allport, G.W. (1961). *Pattern and growth in personality.* New York, USA: Holt, Rinehart and Winston.

Bandura, A. (1977). *Social learning theory.* New Jersey, USA: Prentice Hall.

Bandura, A. (1982). *Model of causality in social learning theory.* Paper presented at the meeting of the Japanese Psychological Association, Kyoto.

Bandura, A. (1986). *Social foundations of thought and action: A social cognitive theory.* New Jersey, USA: Prentice Hall.

Bandura, A., Ross, D., & Ross, S. A. (1963). Imitation of film-mediated aggressive models. *Journal of Abnormal Social Psychology,* **66**, 3-11.

Byrne, R. (2006). *The Secret.* New York, USA: Simon & Schuster.

Cambridge Dictionaries Online. URL: http://dictionary.cambridge.org/ [5 July 2011].

Dayton, L. (2010). *Social support network may add to longevity.* URL: http://articles.latimes.com/2010/sep/13/health/la-he-friends-health-20100913 [28 September 2011].

Dingfelder, S. (2011). Must babies always breed marital discontent? *Monitor on Psychology,* **42** (9), 51.

Dooley, R. (2006). *Non-Verbal Communication and the Brain.* URL: http://www.neurosciencemarketing.com/blog/articles/non-verbal-communication.htm [28 September 2011].

Feist, J. & Feist, G. J. (1998). *Theories of Personality* (4th ed.). Boston, USA: McGraw-Hill.

Helmstetter, S. (1986). *What To Say When You Talk To Your Self.* London, UK: HarperCollins.

Hill, N. (1937/2004). *Think and Grow Rich* (Rev. Ed.). London, UK: Vermilion.

Hogg, M. A. & Vaughan, G. M. (1995). *Social Psychology.* Essex, UK: Prentice Hall.

Institute of HeartMath Research Center. URL: http://www.heartmath.org/research/research-home/research-center-home.html [28 September 2011].

Joseph, J. E. (2009). Neural Correlates of Emotional Reactivity in Sensation Seeking. *Psychological Science,* **20** (2), 215-223.

LeVan, A. (2009). *Seeing is Believing: The Power of Visualization.* URL: http://www.psychologytoday.com/blog/flourish/200912/seeing-is-believing-the-power-visualization [28 September 2011].

Stickgold, R., & Ellenbogen, J. M. (2008). *Sleep on It: How Snoozing Makes You Smarter.* URL: http://www.scientificamerican.com/article.cfm?id=how-snoozing-makes-you-smarter [28 September 2011].

Sweney, M. (2010). *Britons 'watch four hours of TV a day'.* URL: http://www.guardian.co.uk/media/2010/may/04/thinkbox-television-viewing [7 July 2011].

Voss, J. L., & Paller, K. A. (2009). An electrophysiological signature of unconscious recognition memory. *Nature Neuroscience*, **12**, 349-355.

Wikipedia. URL: http://en.wikipedia.org/ [5 July 2011].

Willitts, C. (2011). *Heart Fields*. URL: http://www.mindfulmuscleblog.com/heart-has-consciousness/ [28 September 2011].

Further Increase the Success of Your Relationships

Free Personal Relationship Coaching Consultation

If you are wondering whether you should seek further assistance and simply want to discuss your options, a free, no obligation consultation is available. All one-to-one coaching is strictly confidential, as are any enquiries. For more information, visit www.relationshipscoach.co.uk.

Free Business Relationship Coaching Consultation

The success of any business is based on the success of the relationships between those working within the organisation as well as the organisation and its customers. For more information and a free, confidential, no obligation consultation, visit www.relationshipscoach.co.uk.

Free Monthly Email Newsletter

Keep abreast of useful information to keep you and your relationships growing in the right direction. From insightful information to new research being conducted to motivational quotes, you'll receive a wealth of knowledge. Register within seconds on www.relationshipscoach.co.uk.